To Sandy,

It's wonderful to know you. So many thanks for your support of Youth Aware!

Love,

Roberta Meyer

The Parent
Connection

THE PARENT CONNECTION

How to Communicate with Your Child About Alcohol and Other Drugs

by Roberta Meyer

FRANKLIN WATTS 1984
NEW YORK | LONDON | TORONTO | SYDNEY

The difficulty in acknowledging all those who contributed to this book is that the acknowledgments require another book. Supportive as they are, my publishers just might not go for that, so I'll do my best to keep this to a short story.

Once the idea for the book germinated, I was gently but firmly propelled along by my friend and cohort, Vicki-Marie Peterson. Her ally, Roberta Boomer, prodded me when I flagged. Persis Hamilton, Bill Alexander, Dick Ettinger, Blair Fuller, and Herb Shlosberg gave me invaluable advice on how to begin, how to find an agent, and how to continue in the face of adversity.

Kathy Kirkpatrick introduced me to Carol Costello, whose professionalism, enthusiasm and support are the backbone of the book. Annie Brody, my brilliant agent, appeared at exactly the right moment, through a mutual friend, Beverly Tondreau.

Ben Westheimer, Keven Mahon, and Leif Zerkin contributed their invaluable expertise to the section on alcohol and other drugs.

The quiet manner of my editor, Peggy Tsukahira, along with her eagerness to grasp new concepts about addiction and her ability to clarify my message, were essential components for me.

Don Patterson, Director of Marketing for Franklin Watts, has been the rock of Gibraltar. His initial excitement about the book, his clear explanations of the publishing process, and his ongoing interest have dispelled my initial (and negative) picture of how publishing was supposed to be.

To name all who contributed is impossible, but I particularly want to mention those who are in my training program to become seminar leaders. Each of them contributed valuable time and energy to the book. Without the typing and research skills of Sande Sedgwick, Joanne Kropp, Barbara Sayre, and Diane Boomer, we never would have made our deadlines.

My final acknowledgments and thanks are for my family—my husband, Bill Sheldon, and my daughters, Megan and Deborah Ann. Without their constant encouragement and support not only would this book not have been written, but many others things I have done would never have been accomplished.

Library of Congress Cataloging in Publication Data

Meyer, Roberta.
  The parent connection.

  Includes index.
    1. Children—United States—Alcohol use. 2. Children—
United States—Drug use. 3. Parent and child—United
States. 4. Interpersonal communication—United States.
5. Alcoholics—United States—Family relationships.
I. Title.
HY5133.M49 1984   362.2'92'088054   83-23590
ISBN 0-531-09831-1

Contents

Chapter Three
Telling the Truth   27

The Robot
The Mind
The Observer
What the Truth is *Not*
"There's Something Wrong with Me"
Making Each Other Right and Wrong
Filter Systems
What to Do about Filters
What Is the Truth?
What's in the Way of Telling the Truth?

Chapter Four
Response versus Reaction:
Responding to Our Kids' Reactions   49

Reaction and Response
What Happens When We React
Responding to Our Own Reactions
Responding to Other People's Reactions
Kids Are Going to React. Count on It!
You're Human, Too
Don't Take It Personally
Detachment, Not Desertion
To Be Heard, "Empty the Space"
Escalating Reactions and How to Deal with Them
Leaving versus Commitment

Chapter Five
Parents' Attitudes Meet
Kids' Attitudes. Look Out!   71

Parents' Attitudes
Intention and Attitude

What Is Homeostasis?
How It Works
The Advantages of Homeostasis
The Disadvantages of Homeostasis
The Smiths
Homeostasis in the Family with Alcoholism
Shifting Homeostasis: Losing One's Balance
What to Expect When the Shift Starts
Staying in Communication with Yourself
Dealing with the Unknown

**Chapter Ten
Bad Guys
and Victims   187**

Society's Attitudes about Parents: Guilty!
Society's Attitude about Children: Victims!
Nobody Likes to Feel Guilty
The Guilt/Victim Cycle
Moving from Guilt to Responsibility
To Be a Responsive Parent, Become a Responsive Child
How to Let Go of Blaming Our Parents

**Chapter Eleven
Process   197**

What Is Process?
Our Children's Processes
Competing with Our Children
What Happens When Process Stops
Process for Survival or Aliveness
Mentally Experiencing a Process
Permission versus License
Letting Go of Your Children's Process
Communicating by Example

**Chapter Twelve
Co-ism:
The Ultimate Painkiller   209**

To Ted, Virginia, and Priscilla
for maintaining their faith in me and
to Bill, Megan, and Deborah Ann
for encouraging me to act on that faith.

The Parent Connection

ONE

The Overview: What's Going On Here and Why Does It Look So Strange?

In choosing to read this book, you've accepted a challenge. What goes on between parents and children is one of the most highly charged issues in our society. Alcohol is another. Put them together, and you have a powder keg. In fact, I'm convinced that there's only one way to bring them together without an explosion, and that is through communication.

By communication, I don't mean just talking. You and your children have probably done enough talking at or even with each other to know that words don't produce the kind of human response we all want from communication. We want something more, but we're not sure exactly what it is or how to get it. Sometimes we seem to fall into a rapport accidentally: we try everything we did before and nothing works until suddenly, out of nowhere, we're mysteriously back in communication again. It's quite wonderful—until it once again disappears.

This book is about taking the mystery out of communication without adding another method to our repertoire. This book is about seeing that very often our methods and theories are the very things that keep us out of communication with our children—and everyone else.

I don't think there's a parent alive who doesn't want the best for his or her children. We want them to be happy. We want them to be able to think, choose, and act for themselves—to meet their world with joy and confidence. We also want to be supportive of them, to share with them, to connect with them. And we want a basic human relationship—we want to know that the other person really knows what's going on with us. In return, we want to know what's going on with them.

It's called consciously duplicating one another's experience. When it happens, it's not only a way for both people to understand themselves more deeply and define themselves more clearly; it's also an expression of the love and connection between them.

Sounds terrific, right? Simple, too. So what could go wrong? I'm afraid the answer to that question is "Lots!" In this book, we're going to take apart the process of communication between parents and children, see what could go wrong, and put it back together so that it works. Along the way, we will cover:

- The difference between communicating for the purpose of protecting ourselves from the unknown, proving that we are right and trying to control others, and communicating for the purpose of expanding and enhancing life and love.
- The difference between *responding* honestly and spontaneously to the moment, and *reacting* based on past (and possibly unconscious) beliefs and incidents.
- How filters (judgments, opinions, attitudes, and beliefs) can short-circuit communication if they are not acknowledged, and how telling the truth about them can deepen both our communication with our children and our understanding of ourselves.
- How filters that have to do with alcohol and other drugs can be particularly deadly and even encourage our children to drink or use more drugs than they actually want to.
- How we can help take the "charge" off the issues of alcoholism, alcohol, and other drugs so that our children can make

appropriate choices based on what *they* want, rather than on what we want or don't want.

- How and why "just wanting the best for our kids" often backfires.
- What happens in communication when nobody is the good guy or the bad guy, but when everybody is simply responsible for their own feelings and opinions without presenting them as *The* Truth. What happens when we stop talking about *"The* Truth," and start talking about "my truth" and "your truth."
- How the subtle inner balance most families use to maintain equilibrium, safety, and the status quo can stop communication and keep an alcoholic or addict stuck in the same destructive pattern.
- What happens when the alcoholic upsets this balance by changing, and getting sober.
- The power game of guilt and victimhood between parents and children that's passed from generation to generation—how it's put together.
- How to be a real, genuine person to your children, instead of "the perfect parent," so that they won't have to prove that you made at least one big mistake in your life—them.
- The dynamics of "co-ism," a word used to describe the relationship between the addict and people who build their lives around the addict's "problems" so that they can avoid dealing with their own lives and problems. (Example: Ellen weighed 240 pounds when Joe married her. During their ten-year marriage she gained another 100 pounds, at which point her doctor suggested a stomach bypass operation. Following the operation, Ellen lost 200 pounds and Joe committed suicide. Who had the problem?)
- Why the relationship between parents and children is set up perfectly for co-ism.
- How to let go of your children, to detach from them without deserting them.

▪ The physical properties of alcohol and other drugs—how they affect the mind and body in the long and short term.

▪ Why some people become alcoholics and others who drink just as heavily (or lightly) do not.

▪ An in-depth look at alcoholism—the nature of the disease, early symptoms, who gets it, how it develops, common misconceptions, and communication with alcoholics and co-alcoholics.

▪ What to do if your child is an alcoholic or a co-alcoholic.

Fifteen years as an alcohol educator and counselor have convinced me that communication is the most important factor in dealing with people about their misuse of alcohol. I would even go so far as to say that the alcoholic's ability to recover in a full and satisfying way depends on an ability to communicate with others. I believe that to talk about alcohol and our children without first explaining the communication process is, frankly, a waste of time.

One of the first steps to take when confronted with a child in trouble with alcohol or other drugs is to inform both yourself and your child of the facts. In Part II, I'll outline the facts about alcohol and addiction, and discuss how to apply the communication process in situations involving alcohol and kids.

Finally, since communication between parents and children naturally takes place within the context of the whole family, I also have some things to say about family dynamics: how families relate, interact, and hold together in the crises brought about by drugs—and how you can effect changes in these dynamics if you want to. That's why this book is divided into three parts: Communication, Alcohol, and Family Dynamics.

My hope is that the book's scope will extend far beyond talking with your children about alcohol, and that you will find the information valuable for communicating about everything else as well. I've written specifically for parents of young people ages eleven to eighteen, but most of the information applies also to much younger—and older—children. For the sake of brevity and convenience, I say "alcohol" where, especially in the sections on communication, you can read "alcohol and other drugs." Also for the sake of convenience, I will generally say "he" in many places where I mean "he or she."

THE FIRST STEP

Suppose that one night your daughter Susie, fourteen, comes home an hour after her curfew. As she walks past you up the stairs without offering an explanation, the smell alone makes you feel like you've just drunk two double Scotches. The next morning you have a few words—stern on your part, sullen on hers—and the matter is almost forgotten.

But what's come forcibly to your attention is that over the past several months Susie has changed. For one thing, she doesn't look at all well. Her eyes are red. She seems nervous and tired, anxious and irritable. She's quick to snap at you and the rest of the family, and usually retreats into her room.

She used to bring home A's and B's. Now it's C's and D's. From time to time you've thought that money might be missing from your wallet. She doesn't want to talk about it. You've tried everything, but she just won't respond. The only time she seems remotely happy is when she's with her friends, and she's away from home as much as you'll let her be. Yesterday the school called to tell you she'd shown up drunk for class. When you confronted her, she denied it.

What do you do? Is Susie an alcoholic? If she is, what should you do about it? Or is it just a case of adolescent rebellion, aggravated by what she knows are your suspicions? In any case, how can you get her to open up and talk to you about it? What can you do to help her? And how might you have prevented the situation from escalating to this point?

We will deal with all those questions, but the first thing to do if your child is getting into serious trouble with alcohol or other drugs is to get help. Don't even stop to read this book. You can read it during the time you and/or your child are in therapy or treatment. If your child is undergoing a crisis, get help *now*. These are some national organizations you can contact for help or referrals:

National Council on Alcoholism
733 Third Avenue
New York, New York 10017

Alanon
P.O. Box 182, Madison Square Station
New York, New York 10159

Alcoholics Anonymous
175 Fifth Avenue, Room 219
New York, New York 10010

Tough Love
P.O. Box 70
Sellersville, Pennsylvania 18960

Parents Who Care
703 Welch Road, Suite H4
Palo Alto, California 94304

Even if there isn't a crisis, now is not the time to sit down and suddenly have a heart-to-heart talk with your children about alcohol and other drugs. By now they have all the information they need to know exactly where you stand on this issue—and a lot of others.

Your children know all about you, your beliefs and your reactions to life. They didn't even have to try, and they didn't learn it by the words you used. All they had to do was watch and listen.

They've watched you drink or not drink. They've heard you talk about people who drink and don't drink. They've checked out your medicine cabinet. They know how and why you eat chocolate, smoke cigarettes, bite your nails, withdraw into television. They've seen you react to "drunks," watched you deal with your mother-in-law, observed what goes on between you and your spouse, heard you chastise your sister. They've seen you defend your beliefs, take a stand and stick to it, noticed you compromise, observed you help a neighbor, seen you hug your dad, been with you when you attended church, and heard you criticize their teachers, their friends, and the latest punk rock group.

This is the first principle of communication: *Everything about us communicates—all the time.* Even the things we *aren't aware that we think* get communicated. From this principle, two things are obvious:

1. We can't possibly be honest with our children until we are first honest with ourselves.
2. Things go haywire very quickly if we aren't honest with ourselves, because the truth is being broadcast continually—whether we know it or not, whether we like it or not.

Fortunately, this principle is just as true for our children as it is for us. Just because they don't happen to be talking doesn't mean they aren't telling us about themselves. They are.

THE DRUG OF CHOICE

You probably don't have to be told that alcohol is now the drug of choice among teenagers (and younger children), especially when it is mixed with other drugs. You may also know that half of all teenagers in America drink at least once a month. Lest there be any doubt, however, let's look at some statistics.

> Sixty-six percent of youth in the fourth grade have consumed alcohol at least once. Forty-five percent of youth in the fourth grade considered themselves to be current users of alcohol.
>
> > Social Advocates for Youth study
> > San Francisco Bay Area, 1978

> The Department of Health, Education and Welfare considers alcoholism to be this country's most neglected disease. . . . It is estimated that there are 3.3 million young people who have problems with alcohol. The proportion of teenagers reported to be intoxicated at least once a month rose from 10 percent in 1966 to 19 percent in 1975 . . . (and) over the past four years there has been a 48 percent increase in the number of fifteen-year-olds who had their first drink before the seventh grade.
>
> > *Teenage Drinking*
> > by Robert North and Richard Orange
> > Collier Books, 1980

The National Institute on Alcohol Abuse and Alcoholism's Fourth Report to Congress on Alcohol and Health cites the following statistics:

- There are over ten million alcoholics in the United States.
- 60 percent of reported cases of child abuse involved alcohol.
- 41 percent of reported cases of assault involved alcohol.

- 39 percent of rapes involved alcohol.
- 64 percent of criminal homicides involved alcohol.
- 80 percent of suicides had been drinking.
- 35 to 64 percent of drivers in fatal accidents had been drinking.
- The visible cost to the economy is fifty million dollars per year.

In addition, it is estimated that alcohol is the number one killer in the United States (taking into account its impact on cancer and heart disease, plus specifically alcohol-related deaths such as 25,000 automobile fatalities per year). It is estimated to be the number two source of income for the government (via the liquor sales tax). No wonder there is so much ''charge'' on the subject. No wonder we want our children to know something about it *before* they encounter that first bottle of Boone's Farm Wine.

Add to that the fact that one out of every ten people who drinks is an alcoholic, and you have something you want your kids to know about. But how do you get the information across? How do you let your children realize that they have choices about alcohol and other drugs?

One thing we've learned (and on which nearly everyone agrees) is that kids don't respond well to being lectured. They may hear the information, but it doesn't sink in and become a part of their consciousness.

What does seem to engage young people, or *any* people for that matter, is not so much what you say or how you say it, but your fundamental ''ground of being.'' Whether we are aware of it or not, other people feel what our basic intentions toward them are. If we're communicating to make ourselves look good or to control them, they know it. If we're communicating from support and love, they know it—no matter what we say, and no matter what the ''supposed'' issue is.

If we're not clear ourselves on what our basic attitude is, we will have lots of problems. But looking at that basic attitude honestly and acting accordingly can be our salvation.

WHO'S HELPING WHOM?

When people go out of their way to help others, oddly enough they often learn a lot about themselves. I learned I was an alcoholic by trying to save a friend from *his* problem with alcohol.

When I was a teenager, I danced with the San Francisco Ballet and the New York City Ballet and in that environment had learned quite a bit about drinking and dancing. I found out that, like drinking and driving, the two didn't go well together.

One specific incident in southern California should have given me a clue about my relationship with alcohol. During a performance in a theater-in-the-round, I was supposed to run down the aisle, make my entrance, then run across the stage, and up onto a table top. I did all that and more. After I hit the table top I kept going and landed in the orchestra pit, right in the kettle drum. That should have told me something, but it didn't.

Several years later, I met a wonderful man and we started dating. He was quite special, but there were some very peculiar things about him. On our first date, for instance, he drank thirteen double martinis. I drank seven, but still, he had drunk nearly twice as many as I had. I had thought *I* had a high tolerance, but he could drink me under the table.

Wherever we went together, there was booze. Whether it was a party, or a ballgame, or even the theater, we always went out for a drink or two, and sometimes we didn't make it back for the second act.

He was attractive and smart, went to work every day, and was the youngest vice-president in his bank's history, so he certainly didn't fit my picture of an alcoholic. But he had a habit of forgetting things, such as where we'd been and what we'd done. I wasn't overly concerned—until he started forgetting me.

He'd call to make a date and then he wouldn't show up. Finally I decided to take action.

I marched down to the National Council on Alcoholism in San Francisco and brought home armloads of material to show him that he was an alcoholic and just what he ought to do about it.

As I read the information and underlined his symptoms in red ink, one of the things I learned was that if one person weighs close to two hundred pounds and has thirteen double martinis in him, and another person weighs close to one hundred pounds and has seven double martinis in her, then the one who has had seven double martinis actually has a higher concentration of alcohol in her system than the one who has had thirteen.

Needless to say, I was horrified to realize that he was not the only one with a problem! I began to see that by being with people who drank twice as much as I did, I looked good by comparison. I'd always thought I was lucky because I wasn't one of those girls who threw up in the potted palms, but I learned that a high tolerance to alcohol is one of the early symptoms of alcoholism. I learned a lot of things, including the fact that I was an alcoholic.

The story has a happy ending. That guy turned out to be my husband Bill, and we are both recovered alcoholics with many years of sobriety. But the point is that in trying to help someone else, I discovered that there was a great deal about myself that I needed to look at, and examine, first.

In reading this book, you may not discover that you're an alcoholic, but you will possibly find out more about yourself than you ever dreamed you would.

LOVE

Love is the basis of the kind of communication we'll be talking about. It is the strength behind our efforts to be honest with ourselves and one another, to let ourselves be vulnerable, and to support the other person in being all that he can be. In the process, we're going to have to be all that *we* can be—and love ourselves for it as well.

I don't want to preach at you about your children's relationship to alcohol, or to teach you how to preach at them. This book isn't about temperance, pointing the finger, or trying to fix blame. It's about creating an environment in your family where accurate information can be discussed in a nonthreatening and supportive way; where those who may be suffering from the disease of alcoholism can begin to deal with it; and where young people can learn that they have choices about alcohol and a right to their own life processes, just as you have a right to yours. It's about having the courage to stay connected to one another—to keep communicating even when there is conflict, and even when it seems not to be working.

Sooner or later—probably sooner—your children will catch on. They will understand that you're being more of *you,* and realize that it's all right for them to be more of *them.* Then you'll have something really precious. You and your children will be relating to each other not as adversaries, but as people on the same team who share the goal of communication based not on fear and control, but on love and freedom.

PART I

COMMUNICATION

TWO

Communication:
What It Is and Isn't

I know you're anxious to get right to the good part, to find out exactly how to communicate with your kids about alcohol and other drugs, but be patient. It will take some time because even though communication is incredibly simple, the basis of communication *problems* is complex. Understanding these problems is essential to their eradication, and that groundwork has to be laid before any miracles can take place. Communication is your primary tool for relating to your children—about alcohol, other drugs or anything else—so it's worth taking some time to see just what it is and how it can be used most effectively.

Let's look first at what it isn't.

MISCONCEPTIONS
ABOUT COMMUNICATION

Misconception #1:
True communication is a peak experience.
A lot of us picture two people falling into each other's arms, merging into the "white light" of a "peak experience" and walking into the sunset together. That's like comparing your family to the Waltons. Sometimes communication does involve

peak experiences, but if we're looking for hugs and kisses all the time, we may be disappointed.

Misconception #2:
Communication happens only when
you make a voluntary effort to
verbalize a message to someone.

Actually, we are conveying information about ourselves all the time. Some of the ways we communicate are by words, facial expressions, tone of voice, body language, and even silence. The style and colors of our clothes, our jobs, our cars, our closets, and even our shoes—they're all clues to the person we are.

The minute a thought, a feeling, attitude, or idea forms itself in our mind, it seeks an outlet—a form of expression. Now, I've certainly had some thoughts, feelings, attitudes, and judgments that I'd rather the world didn't know about. In fact, I suspect most of us have had some we'd rather not know we had! That's only human, but in trying to hide them, we pay a price. When those thoughts are left to fester inside, rather than being brought out into the open, they not only do us damage, but they sabotage our voluntary communication. They communicate themselves no matter how hard we try to stop them, so we're only hiding them from ourselves. We think we're communicating one thing, and those hidden or unconscious thoughts and feelings are communicating something else.

This brings us to the third misconception about communication.

Misconception #3:
Communication happens only
between individuals.

Often someone will say to me, ''But no one can know what I'm thinking. You can't tell me what my thoughts are right now, so my thoughts are not being communicated!''

It's true that I can't read your mind. But what you're thinking is a communication—from you to you. In fact, the first person we want to communicate with, *and the main person,* is ourselves. If we start watching where we are, and begin picking up clues about ourselves, we'll have accomplished the first step in successful communication, which is self-honesty. With self-honesty we'll be able to align what we want to communicate with what we are actually communicating.

Communication can and does take place between individuals, but we need to be honest with ourselves about our thoughts, feelings, and attitudes before we can hope to be honest with anybody else. If we're not, they'll know it. And which group of people is most adept at picking up that kind of information? You guessed it. Kids!

Misconception #4
Communication is a two-way street.
Webster's defines communication as "the giving, or the giving and receiving, of information etc. as by talk, gestures, writing, etc." When I first read that definition, some bells rang. It had never occurred to me that communication could be just "giving." I had always self-righteously thought that communication was a two-way street, often saying to myself or someone else, "Well, I can't communicate with him because he just won't listen and he won't communicate back. It takes two to tango." This will rid you of the responsibility of communicating every time. It gets you a scapegoat. But it doesn't get you communication.

Misconception #5:
It's the sender's fault if the
communication doesn't work.
This misconception places the entire burden of seeing that the information gets transmitted completely and accurately on the

person sending the communication. If it succeeds, he can take all the credit. It it fails, it's all his fault. This is great if you're the receiver. All you have to do is sit back, put your feet up, and watch the poor sucker sink or swim. Terrific. Or is it?

The problem with this process is that you have no control over the situation. If you are the receiver, you are completely dependent on the skill of the sender. What if all the people in your life are unskilled senders? Then you simply don't get to receive any communications. There's nothing you can do about it. You may be right, but being right is a poor substitute for communication.

Misconception #6:
It's the receiver's fault if the
communication doesn't work.

Now the shoe is on the other foot. You might be the most brilliant sender in the world, but if all your friends are lousy receivers, too bad. No communication for you. Again, you're at the mercy of someone else's ability or willingness to communicate. They, and not you, are in control of your communication.

What do misconceptions #4, #5, and #6 have in common? In each case, you're out of control. You don't choose whether you're going to be in communication or not—the other person does. If you associate only with expert communicators, people who are thoroughly honest with themselves and with you and who are about a step away from sainthood, then you're in great shape. But if that's not the case, you're out of luck.

What can you do to get back your power, to reclaim the control over your own communication? There's a solution, but you might not like it. It's certainly not fair, but it's terribly effective. It works 100 percent of the time.

THE SOLUTION:
RESPONSIBILITY (NOT BLAME)

The way to take back control is for *you* to be the one who is responsible for the success of the communication, whether you are the sender or the receiver, and whether or not you have an expert communicator for your partner. If you want to communicate effectively, then you be the one to make it happen.

Wait a minute, you say, does that mean I'm to blame for everything? Absolutely not! It isn't a matter of fixing blame. It's simply a matter of what's going to produce the result you want. At the bottom line, the question you have to answer is this: "Do I want someone to blame if it doesn't work, or do I want it to work?"

Blaming the other guy not only takes the focus off our failures in communication, but also tends to take it off the issue we are "trying to communicate about." This is fine, of course, when neither of us is terribly comfortable talking about that particular issue anyway.

Communicating within the framework of responsibility is riskier, but it's also more exciting. It's an adventure into the unknown. It means aiming for expansion rather than protection. It's the difference between going for success and trying to avoid failure.

INTENTION:
LISTENING TO FEEDBACK

Communicating with responsibility means dealing with the issue of intention. Is what's being received the same as what we meant to send? If it isn't, rather than wondering how to make the other person listen, it's usually a good idea to look at what our *real* intention is. Here's an example:

Suppose Charles tells his teenage son, Bobby, that alcohol is less harmful than pot. They get into a serious argument about it, with each one holding tightly to his opinion. The communications Bobby receives are: a) This is just another fight, and Dad's just trying to prove again that he knows more than I do; and b) Dad's trying to tell me alcohol isn't harmful. Naturally, Bobby resists both of these communications.

It's all the more upsetting to Charles, because what he really "meant" to communicate was, "Look, I care about you and I'm concerned about you. Pot isn't the drug of my generation. I don't know much about it and neither does anybody else. Go easy on it." He's concerned about both Bobby and about the unknown factors of the drug, but he can see that Bobby isn't feeling the same concern at all. The message Bobby is getting is that Dad wants to be right and *alcohol is okay.*

For Charles to become responsible for this communication, he must look at it from the perspective that Bobby heard exactly what Charles meant him to hear. In other words, Charles *wanted* Bobby to get the communication that alcohol is okay. The next step is for Charles to look at why he might have wanted Bobby to get that communication. Maybe Charles drinks a lot of alcohol, and wants to justify it somehow to Bobby. Or, maybe he wants Bobby to get the message that he (Charles) is right because he's afraid that as he grows up Bobby is getting to be a little smarter than his father.

What Charles has to do now is figure out whether he wants Bobby to get the message that Dad's right and alcohol's okay, or whether he wants Bobby to get the message that Dad is concerned about him. When Charles makes himself responsible for the communication, and for having intended that Bobby get exactly the message he got, then Charles can go back and choose which communication he really wants to send. And whichever it is, Bobby will get it.

■ ■ ■

I hear a friend say all the time, "I can't understand why Jim's so defensive around me." When I ask her what she thinks of Jim she says, "Well, yes, I think he's a turkey, but I certainly never told him that. In fact, I pay him compliments all the time." Now you tell me. What message is Jim going to get from her? Right. Exactly what she wanted him to get.

How do you know what is being received? The answer is to listen to feedback, verbal or otherwise. Hearing what people "feed back" to you makes you vulnerable. Sometimes it can hurt, but it's the only way to tell what's going on.

This happened to me once when talking to a fifth grade class about alcoholism. I talked for a half hour in a clear and un-biased way about alcoholism. I said that alcoholism is a disease and alcoholics are not bad people. Then, at the end of the session, I asked the class what they had learned. Every child that I called on said "I learned alcoholics are *terrible* people."

I can shake my head and say I never said that, and can't imagine how they got that idea, but that's what I communicated. If I'm going to be responsible for my communication, I have to realize that and look at the reasons why I may have wanted to convey that message. Perhaps, in this case, I was more upset about my alcoholic neighbor losing control and kicking my dog than I had been willing to admit.

Being responsible about receiving feedback means taking the point of view, whether you actually believe it or not, that what people receive is exactly what you *meant* them to receive. When it comes to intention in communication, it doesn't matter at all what you said. *It only matters what they heard.* Only by apply-ing self-honesty in this way can you begin to figure out what is keeping your communication from working, and where to begin changing it.

On the surface, especially at first, being responsible for your intention seems like a bum rap. How come you have to be responsible, while everybody else can just sit back? The answer, of course, is that you don't have to be responsible. You don't have to look at your true intentions. The point is, do you want your communication to work? Believe me, the effect that being responsible for your communication will have is that it will begin to work in a hurry.

COMMUNICATION IS THE DUPLICATION OF EXPERIENCE

True communication requires the ability to duplicate experience. By that I mean being able and willing to set aside your own opinions or feelings long enough to truly hear what another is telling you, verbally or otherwise.

One of the primary purposes of this book is to explore what hinders our ability to duplicate another's experience, and to see what stands in the way of duplicating our experience for them. Duplicating someone's experience is *not* the same as understanding it.

Understanding may be better than nothing, but not much. It's what we settle for when we don't know how to duplicate. Unfortunately, most communication takes place at the level of understanding.

Understanding is what happens when you compare a past experience of your own to the experience someone else is narrating, and say "I know exactly how you feel. I felt just the same way when . . ." Understanding means you can only communicate if you think you've had an experience similar to someone else's.

Duplication comes from a deeper "knowing" which recognizes that *all* experience is *one* experience. This is why there have been times when you felt most "understood" when no words were spoken. You weren't being understood. You were being duplicated. The other person simply "got" what your experience was, and you knew it.

Duplication of experience requires only one thing: conscious intention. This entails the willingness to let go of thought patterns, beliefs, and feelings, to intend to hear the other's experience, and to have them hear yours.

There are no rules for duplication. It is not a method, though there are those who have tried to make it one. As soon as something is turned into a method, it becomes technical. Believe me, nothing will create a greater resistance to communication than the idea that one is being subjected to a technique.

HOW TO TAKE RESPONSIBILITY

Communication can take place either within a framework of consciousness, responsibility, and risk, or in a framework of blame, manipulation, and protection. The latter is safer. We can always make a good argument that the other guy is to blame. Manipulating people is easier than listening to what they're communicating and what they're hearing from us. However, it's not much fun. And you miss the experience of mastery in your life and your communication, honesty, excitement, joy, intimacy, freedom, and love.

How do you take the leap from one framework into the other? How do you go about "taking responsibility"? One way is to remember that responsibility is a "be" rather than a "do," a context in which you hold your communication, "a place you come from."

There are, however, some very basic and simple things you can do to take responsibility for your communication. The first is not to take being responsible too seriously.

Don't be the victim of responsibility.

When people first hear about the idea of responsibility in communication, they sometimes feel as though it's too difficult to even contemplate. They experience responsibility as a great weight, a burden they'll have to carry for the rest of their lives. "Now I'm going to have to be really careful about everything I think, do, and say!", they moan. In fact, it means just the opposite. Being responsible means being responsible for what you *are now,* not for what you "should" be. It means letting down barriers, not putting up new ones. It means being willing to tell the truth, hear the truth, and respond to it.

Life is much easier if you realize that everything about you is communicating automatically, so you might as well relax and enjoy it.

Understand that communication is not talking.

Sometimes people think that if they are talking with their children, they are communicating, and if they're not talking, they're not communicating. You can talk all night without communicating, and you can be in deep and total communication without any words at all. Remember, it's not the words that communicate; it's your intention.

Simply reach out and take responsibility, deliberately and consciously.

Responsibility isn't some mysterious thing to which you have to be initiated. It's a context, a framework, within which you can hold your life and your communication. All that's required is that you: a) want to respond; b) take the point of view that you are the one who is responsible for the success of the communication; and c) realize that people are going to receive exactly what you want them to receive.

Understand "response-ability."

The Latin word "sponsor" means "to answer to," but "sponsor" comes from the deeper root word "spons," which means free will. Responsibility is, therefore, the ability to answer to a situation of the moment, using free will. We don't have to react automatically based on the past.

Tell the truth.

This may be the most important thing about taking responsibility. We can't possibly be responsible if we aren't being honest with ourselves. Telling the truth means much more than simply not lying. That's why the whole next chapter is devoted to telling the truth.

THREE

Telling the Truth

There's something very simple about telling the truth. You don't have to think about it or try and figure it out. You don't have to add anything to what's already there. You don't even have to be afraid of it. Hiding the truth about reality isn't going to make reality any better, and it might make it a whole lot worse. Why, then, don't people tell the truth all the time? The answer has to do with some conflicting parts of ourselves.

THE ROBOT

One of the main barriers to telling the truth is the Robot. The Robot is that part of us that reacts when our buttons are pushed. It's the part of us that goes "on automatic" when we hear, see, or feel something we'd rather not experience.

When we start talking about the Robot in workshops, the participants have a tendency to nod off and go to sleep. Or they get bored, restless, hungry, or have to go to the bathroom. Their Robots will do anything to avoid hearing what's being said. As you read this chapter, you may find yourself doing some of those same things. You may get confused, or angry, or anxious, or bored. That's fine. Just remember it's only your Robot that's having a little trouble with all this, and not you!

We all know that there is a part of us that supports our well-being and a part of us that doesn't. Think back to the last time you said you were going on a diet. You did fine for a few days, until you went home for Christmas. There were all sorts of goodies and happy childhood memories. But then you got to thinking about Christmases past when you used to look at your fat old Aunt Sally and swear you'd never look like her. And now here you are, the same age as she was then, only you weigh twenty pounds more than she did. You start feeling so awful that you pop another piece of fruitcake in your mouth.

That's the part that sabotages you, the part that doesn't support you in having what you really want, which is to lose weight. There are lots of names for that part of us, but we will be calling it the Robot. The Robot is made up of our thoughts and our feelings, but is run by our *Mind*.

THE MIND

Our Mind's functions are to judge, evaluate, compare, decide, analyze, compute, and figure things out—all based on the past. In a way, our Mind is like a giant memory bank or file cabinet. Whenever it encounters a new stimulus, it rushes back to the file to find something similar. If our Mind perceives a fire, for example, it will race back to the "Fire" file and find that you don't stick your hand into a fire because it will burn you, causing great pain. That's a valuable piece of information. Our Mind has fulfilled its function. It has saved the Robot.

However, our Mind has a desperate need to know exactly what is going on all the time, and to be right about the things it knows. So even if the new stimulus isn't really the same as what's in the file cabinet, our Mind will say that it is. That's where it starts getting us into trouble, especially where communication is concerned. We've all witnessed "discussions" over the most insignificant things that have resulted in fisticuffs, or the end of a close relationship. These are examples of our Mind fighting for its survival at great cost to the individual.

"What's wrong with survival?" people ask. Nothing's wrong with survival when you're talking about avoiding car crashes, but it's not a very enlivening context in which to hold your life. Living for survival means that everything you do stems from a fear of death, loss, separation, failure, etc. Conversely living within a context of aliveness means embracing life, accepting it, going toward it, which includes embracing the possibilities of death, loss, separation, and failure as well. Survival is oriented toward avoidance; it constricts, hampers and diminishes. Aliveness is oriented toward acceptance and enhancement; it expands and enriches.

THE OBSERVER

There's another part of us that *does* support our well-being. Fortunately, it is even stronger than our Mind. It is called the Observer—or the experiencer, the soul, the spirit, the watcher, the witness, whatever word you want to use for it. The Observer's real power is that it doesn't fear anything; it is free to love and to trust. It sees through everything to our essential perfection.

The Observer recognizes that our ability to experience all of ourselves—both the things our Minds have decided are "good" and the things our Minds have decided are "bad"—is what allows us to expand and fulfill ourselves, to live in a context of aliveness. The Mind is a noisy, know-it-all, yet uncertain voice; the Observer is a quiet, certain feeling which never has to "prove" itself. Understanding another's experience is a function of the Mind; duplicating another's experience is a function of the Observer.

A woman in one of my seminars discovered her Observer

through the following experience. She had spent many months worrying about her daughter's suspected use of marijuana. She had no proof, however, and so dared not say anything. She clearly remembered her rage at her own mother's apparent lack of trust in her as a teenager. So she continued to fret, worry, and keep quiet. Needless to say, her Robot was going nuts.

Then one day, following the seminar, she *noticed* that she was worrying. She *noticed* that she was unwilling to say anything to her red-eyed, listless daughter. She suddenly realized that she didn't have to "prove" to her that she was a "modern" mother, or that she trusted her. She saw that her need to be right and her unwillingness to confront her daughter's behavior were not helping either of them. For the first time, however, she saw all of this from a quiet, unthreatened part of her. The Observer was noticing, instead of the Robot judging. And, also for the first time, she was able to describe to her daughter two things: a) the things she observed in her daughter's behavior and appearance; and b) her own reaction to those things. Her daughter was so relieved that something had finally been said that she burst into tears and confessed that she was truly frightened by her lack of motivation and wanted some kind of help. There's no guarantee that this will happen for you, but it is true that operating from the Observer vantage point makes it much easier for others to do the same.

As you read this book certain statements, anecdotes, and examples will activate your Robot. The part of you that can watch that reaction without blaming either you or the book for the reaction is the Observer.

WHAT THE TRUTH IS *NOT*

Five things commonly mistaken for the truth are: judgments, decisions, stuffing, dumping, and viewpoints. It may seem obvious to you that these things aren't the truth, but if you give it some thought you may find that about 95 percent of what passes for the truth are actually these very things. Let's take them one at a time.

Judgments are not the truth.

Judgments aren't bad; they're just not the truth. They are final conclusions based on subjective values, and they are quite different from observations. A judgment would be, "That kid is a sick drug addict and a drunk." An observation would be, "That kid has needle tracks on his arms, smoked three joints when he was over on Saturday, drank a six-pack of beer and looked like he hadn't touched a drop. According to the texts I've read, those are symptoms of abnormal use of alcohol and other drugs." Judgments are just another way of making ourselves right.

Take the case of Jackie and Fred Smith, and their sixteen-year-old son, Fred, Jr. Jackie has the judgment that no one under the age of eighteen should ever taste booze. Fred has the judgment that "the boy has to learn to handle his liquor." With a set of judgments like that in the house, chances are it's only a matter of time before Fred, Jr. goes out and gets roaring drunk.

Sure enough, one night he comes home and he's walking into walls. Jackie and Fred jump on him, each screaming their judgments. Then an odd thing happens: instead of screaming at Fred, Jr., Jackie and Fred begin screaming at each other. Fred, Jr. sees his chance and slips upstairs. Jackie and Fred aren't talking about him anymore. They're not even talking about drinking. *They're talking about whose judgment is right* and whose Robot is going to be in control. They're on "automatic," and have lost touch with the Observer and their true intention, which is their concern for Fred, Jr.

The point is not to stop judging, or to castigate ourselves when we do judge. The point is simply to observe when we have made a judgment, and remember that it's not the truth.

Decisions are not the truth.

The word "decide" comes from the same root word as suicide, homicide, matricide, etc., which mean to kill or murder. When the Mind decides something, for example, that alcohol is good and marijuana is bad, it is "murdering" any possible alternatives. (The Mind, remember, likes to know what is going on and to be right.) The Mind that has made this decision will find it hard to bend, even if the FDA proves that marijuana could be of assistance to those with glaucoma or undergoing chemotherapy. And, though alcohol causes serious damage to millions, this Mind will say something like "alcohol has been around for thousands of years—we might as well live with it."

One way we know for sure that decisions aren't the truth is that our minds can and do make conflicting decisions. For example, ever since Cindy's father had his third DWI (Driving While Intoxicated) arrest, and her mother's reaction culminated in her hospitalization for a nervous breakdown, Cindy has decided that "men who drink alcohol will drive you insane." At the same time, she likes her father only when he has some alcohol in him—he's too irritable otherwise. So, the other decision she made is that "men are pleasant only when they've been drinking alcohol." With those two decisions operating, Cindy hasn't much chance of a successful relationship with a man! This would be a good time for Cindy to remember that she isn't only her Mind; she can detach herself and evaluate the decisions it makes.

If you're trying to communicate with a child you've already decided is a sullen troublemaker who takes after your brother-in-law, and you've "murdered" the alternative that he could be anything else, you'll have some problems with communication. Your "anti-sullen" Robot is now in a power struggle with his "sullen Robot." Someone has to end up right, unless someone moves out of Robot Land into response.

Stuffing and dumping are not the truth.

Stuffing and dumping? It sounds like a new dance, but these are just a few more ways we try to make ourselves right and protect ourselves.

Long ago, when we were children, some of us decided that our emotional responses to situations were very often inappropriate. When we cried because Aunt Jane didn't give us what we wanted for our fourth birthday, it made everybody upset. We decided that crying was an inappropriate response to that situation, even if we felt like crying. Later, we decided just to pretend we were happy and hope the hurt would go away.

Thus, one of the first things we learned to do with our emotional responses was to stuff them down and not let them show. Now, after all these years, it's almost second nature. We come up against the child-with-bad-report-card, and instead of expressing how concerned and upset we feel, Robot "good parent" tries to be "calm" and "reasonable."

Interestingly enough, our mate may react in a totally different manner, which we consider unreasonable or "off the wall." He dumps. It may be hard to believe, but *his* dump may be an expression of *our* anger.

Dumping is the other side of the coin. Instead of stuffing emotional reactions down inside yourself, you spew them all over everybody in sight. You may cry, and moan, and wail. You may also be more subtle, keeping a stiff upper lip, refusing to talk about the terrible lot that life and your kids have dealt you, and make everyone around you miserable. (In that case, the stuff is really a dump.)

Another way I can dump is to let my anger out, but imply that it's all someone else's fault. "I'm furious with my daughter for getting drunk last night and smashing up the car. In fact I'm so upset I couldn't even go to work today." Who could blame me for that? The implication is if it weren't for her, then I'd be able to get to work.

Contrary to popular belief, dumping doesn't work—for your health or for any other purpose. People often think that ventilating negative feelings diminishes them. Acutally, releasing them just makes them worse. Stuffing them, of course, does the same thing. So what do we do with this swirling sea of emotions? There are viable alternatives to dumping and stuffing. They are *experiencing* and *expressing,* and they are done by the Observer.

Experiencing might look a little like stuffing on the surface, because it can be done internally and nobody need even see it. I might stand up in front of a room full of people, for instance, feeling extremely nervous. I might have physical sensations, a pounding heart, an upset stomach, and sweaty palms, yet I still can look calm. Telling the audience about it would be dumping my discomfort on them. Instead, I can go ahead with my speech, recognizing that I'm experiencing these sensations. Later I can duplicate the experience for my husband, thereby expressing my feelings and also releasing the energy I used to control my nervousness.

To experience, simply observe what happens when you come into contact with a certain stimulus, without judging it or making decisions about it or classifying it as good or bad, right or wrong. Let yourself feel whatever you are feeling completely, and then choose what you want to do about it. When you are upset, you can respond. You do not have to react.

Viewpoints are not the truth.

Imagine that you are one of four people facing outward in a circle in the center of your living room. Each of you is asked to describe the room, based only on what is seen from his or her vantage point. The result will be four very different descriptions.

Now imagine that each of you have to get the others to agree with you about what the room looks like, based only on your viewpoint, as if you had never seen any other part of the room.

Then pretend you're talking about life, rather than the living room, and you see why communication goes awry when viewpoints are presented as truth.

In order for us to see the whole room, we have to get out of whatever position we're in so that we can see from the positions of the other people. To get an even more accurate picture of the room, we would need many more viewpoints. The reason it's difficult for us to see that our viewpoints are not the truth is that we can see the view, but we can't see the point from which we view it, because we *are* that point.

The same thing happens in families. One person is looking at a situation from the position of being fifteen years old. One sees it from the position of the alcoholic; another from the position of a nondrinker. This isn't much of a problem, unless we've decided our positions are *right* and we start to present them as The Truth. "I'm a Republican, and that's right." "I'm a Catholic, and that's right." It's not that being a Republican or a Catholic is right, it's just that it works for *you*. That doesn't mean it's right for everyone.

Communication involves being bigger than our own individual points of view. Suppose that Ann and Mike go to a movie together. Ann has one point of view about it, and Mike has another. They can argue about who is right, which will limit their experience of the movie, or they can see one another's point of view, which would enhance their individual experiences. Neither has to compromise. Neither has to give up anything. Neither loses. In fact, they each gain. They each still have their own experience of the movie, and one another's besides. And neither one is diminished through the exchange.

What happens in families when parents treat their personal viewpoints as the only truth? With children, one of two things happen. Either they abdicate from making their own choices, and adopt all their elders' viewpoints, which means they have no true self-chosen foundation, or they rebel and put an enormous amount of energy into proving that their parents' viewpoints are not only untrue, but dead wrong.

Sometimes people say, "But if I'm not right, what am I?" You are you, and you can't improve on that by being "right" about something. We need to understand that *we are not our viewpoints*. We are the choosers of our viewpoints; we choose the point from which we view. If we think we are our viewpoints, then we're going to be very upset when someone attacks them. We'll think they are attacking us. That means that anyone who doesn't agree with us is the enemy.

Here's an example of how neither of two opposing views is right or wrong, but only becomes unworkable when right or wrong is imposed on the situation. In cultures in which wine is served with meals—not because it's right or wrong to do so, but just because it is the custom—the children don't have a high incidence of problem drinking. The same is true in families where wine isn't served, not because it's right or wrong, but just because they don't choose to serve it. In families where no alcohol is served because it's wrong to do so, or in families where alcohol is given to children to protect the parents' drinking habits, there is a high incidence of problem drinking. (We'll make the distinction between alcoholism and problem drinking later. For now, it's enough to know that alcoholism is a disease, and problem drinking is a condition which has psychological roots.)

"THERE'S SOMETHING WRONG WITH ME"

If judgments, decisions, stuffing, dumping, and viewpoints aren't The Truth, then where do they come from? Often, they start with the viewpoint that "There's something wrong with me." This viewpoint isn't something that just pops up from time to time and disappears. It's a pervasive, negative ground of being that underlies nearly everything else in our lives. It's the Robot's foundation.

We try to find lots of reasons for it. We say "My nose is too big," or "I'm too selfish." We think that if we get our nose fixed, or become more generous, or lose weight, then things will be just fine, but they never are. We still don't feel okay. Finally, after we've done everything there is to do and we still think there's something wrong with us, we start putting it off on the other guy.

If parents have spent fifteen, twenty, twenty-five years trying to fix themselves but still feel as though there's something wrong, then they'll start trying to fix their kids. At least then they'll be okay as parents. When it doesn't turn out the way they think it should, as it never does when they are doing it for that reason, the results are devastating.

To combat the sneaking feeling that "something's wrong with me," we sometimes try to set up our lives so that we will be right—or at least not so wrong as the other guy. "The other guys" can be alcoholics, working mothers, nonworking mothers, Democrats, Communists, Blacks, Whites, anyone who is "other."

Our kids, of course, will try the same thing, with us as the "other." To relate to them, we have to be willing to realize that in their eyes we may seem to have worse problems than they think they have. But we aren't going to lose our kids' respect, just because we have a few faults. We're more apt to lose it by pretending we have none. Or, as in one case I worked with, the child felt so inferior to her "perfect" parents, she had a nervous breakdown before she was twenty. Her parents' perfection did nothing to enhance her well-being.

MAKING EACH OTHER
RIGHT AND WRONG

There are many versions of the right/wrong game. Some of them are "I'm okay; you're not okay," "I can do anything better than you," one-upmanship, and "gotcha." Any kind of manipulative power game in which one person is "better than," and another is "worse than," is a form of the right/wrong game.

To the extent that any of these games are going on, communication cannot be effective because the real message is "I'm right and you're wrong." And that's what's being communicated; not the message. It's purpose is to protect the Robot—the part of us that reacts.

On the other hand, when the communication comes from the Observer, out of aliveness and the willingness to take risks, then the communication is just itself. There is no hidden message; there is just communication. And that's what we're out to achieve.

Judgments, opinions, attitudes, decisions, and labels are all things the Robot uses to make itself right, and other people wrong. I had a friend who was always saying, "Men are such jerks! If I could find one who wasn't, I'd marry him." She never did get married because every time she found a man who wasn't a jerk she'd manage to have him leave her. This proved, of course, that men are jerks. That kind of decision limits your experience of people, but you do get to be right.

You can also make yourself right by being inadequate or awful. I did. My father had graduated Phi Beta Kappa at the age of nineteen. My mother was second in the California Nursing Board Examinations. My sister was tested and declared a superior child at the age of three. To distinguish myself, I had to be the inadequate one, the neurotic one, the problem child. The implication was that they had somehow made me feel inadequate. That's not the truth, but I had everybody, even my psychiatrist, buying it and it worked beautifully. My attitude, unconscious as it may have been, was "I'll show them they're not that great (they're wrong). No family that great would have a dummy like me in it. I'll make them all look stupid! (I'm right.)"

The need to be right and its accompanying postures—defensiveness and self-righteousness, even claims of inadequacy—these are all ways of avoiding responsibility. It's something to watch out for in yourself as well as in your children. If someone thinks they're not self-righteous because they're always wrong, look again.

Sometimes when we talk about how the right/wrong game makes communication difficult, if not impossible, parents will protest, "But what about ethics? What about morals?!" We're not talking about a situation in which there are no ethics or about letting your kids go out and create havoc in the world. This will be clearer as we move through the book. For now, we're just talking about avoiding a "game" that makes it impossible for us to communicate with our kids effectively, or for them to communicate with us.

FILTER SYSTEMS

Our filter systems are the composite of all our decisions about the way we are, the way other people are, and the way the world is. These decisions (judgments, opinions, viewpoints, attitudes, beliefs, and labels) arose from our fear of experiencing things we have decided we would rather not experience. They were made at threatening or dangerous times in our life, and they are rarely conscious decisions. If they were, they'd be a lot easier to deal with because we could see them.

The filter system's purpose is to make reality seem known and familiar to us, so that we can avoid facing the unknown or seeing parts of ourselves we would rather not see. The filter system is protective and it does its job very well.

If I have a filter, for instance, that says that alcoholics are bums who hang out in gutters clutching bottles of wine, then I'm certainly not going to recognize the alcoholic who's wearing a three-piece suit and sitting behind a desk. I may not want to, either, because he may be related to me. In fact, he may even *be* me. With my filter in place, I don't have to see anything. I avoid—or rather, postpone—the pain.

Here's an example of a more subtle filter. If I've made the decision that I'm lazy, then I can lean back and relax. No one expects any more from me, and I don't expect any more from myself. The filter system impacts not just on me, but on everybody else. As dreadful as I am, they all have to be worse so I can be right. So what's worse than being lazy? Being an overly ambitious, money hungry, capitalistic egomaniac. The world is filled with them and I can always say, well I may be laid-back, but at least I'm not doing all the damage those guys are! Remember, of course, the scenario can be equally well played in reverse!

Groups and societies have filter systems, too, just as individuals do. Capitalists have filters about Communists. Communists have filters about Capitalists. Republicans have filters about Democrats and vice versa. Everybody has filters about everybody. We try to gather around us as much agreement as we can for whatever filter system we've set up, so that we can be even more right than we were before. "Group right" is a lot more comfortable than dealing with all those filter systems that are threateningly different from ours.

Unfortunately, the system backfires. Our lives become filled with people mirroring back to us the things we're trying most desperately to avoid. We become magnets for everything that bothers us, and the worst of it is—so does everybody else! The result is a large network of interlocking filter systems, in which everybody is drawing to them exactly the qualities they like least. This is why the world sometimes looks so crazy. It is.

Here's a happy story of a girl who caught her filter system in action.

I gave a talk at a high school one day about the tendency of people who grow up in alcoholic homes to be attracted to alcoholics and marry them. After the talk, one of the girls came up with eyes as big as saucers and thanked me. She said she'd been about to break up with her boyfriend that very night. She'd decided he didn't love her because he never brought her presents or flowers. She realized during the talk that she has a filter that said, "If a man really loves you, he'll give you lots of presents." Her father had always showered her with presents and given her anything she wanted. What she had forgotten was that her father was an alcoholic and had always given her all those presents right after he'd been on a binge and was feeling guilty.

She had been on the verge of ending her relationship so she could find someone just like her father who brought her presents. What she now realized was that such a man quite possibly would have brought them for the same reason—because he was an alcoholic and felt guilty. When she could step back from her filter system and observe it, she didn't have to be blinded by it. She could stay with her boyfriend even though he didn't bring her presents.

Human beings have sensitive antennae. If your filter matches my filter, we'll find each other out of all the billions of people in the world. Not only will we find each other, but our coming in contact with one another may activate a filter that's been latent for twenty years. The story of Mary and Joe is a good example.

Joe's mother was an alcoholic, and as a child he grew up in a household that was in constant turmoil. His mother was unpredictable. He never knew when she would be home, so they could never make any plans. The men she married were often violent, and from time to time bad fights broke out. But Joe's mother could be so sweet, pretty, and witty that Joe loved her completely, even though he couldn't count on her for anything.

Joe made some powerful decisions. One of them was that pretty women with big brown eyes couldn't be trusted. Another was that violence was out; he wouldn't have it in his life. He became a pacifist, wouldn't go to Vietnam, and had a basically even disposition.

Mary's childhood trauma was of a quite different order. One day when Mary was very little and her parents were on vacation, she was out in the baby carriage with the nurse. All of a sudden out of the blue, a huge, bushy, black dog leapt into the buggy, bit Mary, and then just disappeared. The nurse was so horrified that she never told Mary's parents about it. She covered the incident up and everybody forgot about it.

About twenty years later, grown-up Mary goes out to a party. She sees a guy sitting across the room, takes one look at him and . . . *bad vibes*. Bushy, black beard. She doesn't know why, but she doesn't want anything to do with him.

Meanwhile, he's looking at her. She has huge brown eyes and he says to himself, "She's really pretty, but . . ." *Again, bad vibes*. Later, though, after a couple of drinks and a joint, he decides to get acquainted. They start talking and discover they like each other. They both forget their bad vibes and don't even talk about how they didn't like each other on first sight.

They begin seeing one another and after a while their relationship seems so wonderful, they decide to get married. About three weeks after the wedding, Joe is waiting for Mary to come home. She said she'd be home at 6:00 and it's already 10:00. Joe is starting to feel strange—very strange. He hasn't felt this way in a long time, so long he can't remember when. He's starting to get angry. He's never been upset this way with anyone. As it gets later and later he's so full of rage that he's actually scared.

At about 10:30, Mary comes in. She tells him about a flat tire and many other plausible delays. Finally they smooth it over. Four weeks later, she doesn't come home until midnight. This time Joe is livid with rage, but when Mary tells him she ran out of gas, he calms down and everything's fine. Three weeks later, Mary comes in at 2:00 A.M. This time Joe doesn't even listen to her excuses. He is so enraged he explodes . . . and *he bites* her.

Couldn't happen, right? Want to bet?

The lesson here is not that both Joe and Mary should have trusted their "bad vibes" instincts. Very often what we think are our instincts or gut reactions are only our filter systems. The lesson is that our filters are so powerful that we can cause another person's complementary filter to do the very thing that we've already unconsciously decided they will do.

When you introduce the element of alcohol into the filter system, the magnet seems to get even stronger. Sometimes it seems as though 90 percent of alcoholics are people whose main goal in life was never to be like their father or their mother, who was an alcoholic. The problem isn't so much alcohol as it is Dad or Mom. That's one way alcoholism becomes a disease of denial. If I'm an alcoholic, that means I'm like Dad. I can't be like that; therefore, I can't admit that I'm an alcoholic.

Filter systems are so subtle, so innocuous, we rarely recognize that they're there. It's like looking at an optical illusion. We think we're seeing reality and don't question it but we really aren't seeing what's there at all.

WHAT TO DO ABOUT FILTERS

Let the Observer notice when your Robot goes into action. This means your filters are up. Acknowledge that what you're thinking or feeling may not be based on an absolute truth. Then you are in a position to choose. Do you want to keep the filter and be safe, or put it aside and take a risk? If you choose to put it aside, then all you have left is yourself. That is a more desirable place from which to communicate than from your filters. Communication is, among other things, the ability to get past all those filters so that you are in communication with yourself. If you aren't in communication with you, how can anyone else be?

Watch out, though. Letting go of your filter system will put you right in the middle of the unknown. This may be so uncomfortable that things might seem to be getting worse instead of better. It might seem that you're more judgmental and afraid than you ever dreamed you could be. That's only because you're more aware of your judgments and fears. That's progress. The more aware you are of what those judgments and fears are, the better you'll be at handling them.

When you understand that you have a filter system, come to recognize when you start using it, and learn to set it aside, then you have the opportunity to really start trusting your instincts and your intuition. Because you know what your filter system is and how to deal with it, you don't have to be concerned that you're confusing your intuition with your filters.

WHAT IS THE TRUTH?

We know what the truth is not, but what is it? The truth is reality, but what's that? People have been wrestling with that question forever, and the best answer anyone has come up with is that *reality is whatever you perceive it to be*—filters and all. Whatever you think is real, that's what's real for you. The more we are in touch with the Observer, the more our truth approaches what we might call on "absolute" truth. But unless we are freed of all our filters (an impossiblity), we will always be dealing with a truth that is filtered to some degree. Our goal is not to get rid of all our filters, but to let the Observer notice them as often as possible.

Reality changes according to external factors. Hundreds of years ago, reality was a flat earth. Reality was once a sun that revolved around the earth. Everyone agreed on these things then, but of course times and realities change. Hardly a day goes by that scientists don't discover something about our physical universe that's entirely different from the way we thought it was.

That ought to make us a little more humble, a little more flexible about our definition of reality.

Because realities differ from time to time and from person to person, it's nearly impossible to tell "The Truth." Each of us can only know the truth for ourselves. If we're going to try to communicate with one another, it will work a lot better if we each recognize that we see things from our own individual perspective, that we have past decisions and filters that are still operative, that some part of us is going to want to try and be right about them, and that we each have our own truth.

Sometimes the mind tricks us into thinking that a strong filter system ensures a strong reality, when actually just the opposite is true. Our filter systems diminish our reality because we operate from viewpoints that are based on the past, rather than opening up to include new and constantly expanding realities based on the present.

There are some universal Truths, laws of the universe that govern everything. In order to get to those Truths, however, we have to be willing to address our own personal truths.

WHAT'S IN THE WAY
OF TELLING THE TRUTH?

It seems so simple to tell the truth, and on one level it is. But on another level, telling the truth is frightening. Our minds and filter systems have been around for decades, and old habits die hard. There are all sorts of reasons for not telling the truth, but these are some of the ones most apt to be in the way when we're communicating with our children.

Fear of being judged and criticized.
This is a well-grounded fear. It may very well happen. Telling the truth about your filters will remind other people of *their* fil-

ters. That's the last thing they want and, in fact, since they may not have made the choice to look at and tell the truth about their filters, there's some justification for their anger. The trick is not to "make them wrong" for their filters, but simply to tell the truth about your own. For example:

Susan told her son that she realized her reactions to his attending rock concerts were based on a filter that said, "Kids don't really care about the music—what they really want is an excuse to get stoned." She admitted the filter was based on her own experience as a chocolate junkie who often said she really enjoyed grocery shopping, when the truth was she just wanted an excuse to buy Hershey bars. She expected him to be pleased with her confession.

Instead, he just became more sullen than ever. Why? Because, *he* had a filter that said, "A rock concert isn't a rock concert without dope." Unwittingly, she had revealed it. In addition, she had taken responsibility for her own filter (which her son had been aware of ever since he started finding half-eaten chocolate bars hidden under the dishtowels). It had now become harder for him to fool himself and to continue trying to fool her. No wonder he was angry!

Fear of losing our children's respect.
This is a deep one, because we think if we lose our children's respect, then we lose our children.

Before she spoke up, Susan had thought, "What will he think of me if I tell him the truth?" "Not much," whispered her Mind, the part of her that didn't think she was all right the way she was, and was afraid she might be even worse than she suspected.

We forget that our kids know all about us anyway, so there's nothing to be gained from lying and everything to be gained from telling the truth.

Fear of losing our own self-respect.

If we have to look at all those filters, what on earth are we going to think of ourselves?

If our kids can figure it out, don't you suppose there's some part of us that knows we have all those "awful" things? And don't you suppose that, even beyond that, there's a part of us that sees our fine, true selves behind the filters? That's the Observer, the part of us that keeps us growing and moving, that keeps impelling us toward the risky, dangerous, unknown things 'so that we can confront them and go beyond them to our wholeness and completion. That's the part of us we want to identify with, not the Robot.

The Observer is a lot more powerful than we think. If you doubt its power, remember how often it wins over the Mind and brings uncomfortable things into your life to be experienced and handled.

Fear of being WRONG.

This, obviously, is the worst thing that could happen. It's the Mind's greatest fear. If the Mind is to survive, it has to be right.

All the fears we've discussed come out of the survival mentality, out of the decisions we've made, and out of our reactions based on the past rather than out of responses in the present. In the next chapter, we'll talk about the difference between reacting out of the past and responding in the present, what that means to our communication with our children, and how we can respond when our children are reacting.

FOUR

Response vs. Reaction:
Responding to
Our Kids' Reactions

REACTION AND RESPONSE

Reaction comes from the Robot/Mind and response from the Observer. Response is a reply based on the experience of the present moment. Reaction is based on the past. It means to "act again," or "to go back to a former condition." Most of the things we talked about in the last chapter—filters, decisions, judgments—have to do with reaction.

When we react, something out of the past has been reactivated and we go on "automatic." The Robot lives! The Mind reaches right back into the file cabinet and starts making decisions and murdering alternatives. Most of our reactions are unconscious; we react without realizing that we've done so.

Alcoholism is a subject that triggers strong reactions. Sally blames her alcoholic mother for her miserable childhood. When Sally has children of her own, there are two ways she might deal with the subject of drinking. One way is to react; the other is to respond. Here's what the two results might be:

Reaction: Sally's mother was an alcoholic. Sally doesn't want her children to suffer the same fate. In reaction, she forbids them to drink. Being kids, they react. Not realizing that their mother's prohibition comes out of her love and fear for them, they rebel. One of them is an incipient alcoholic. Of course, he hides it and lies about it. He wouldn't want his mother to be right. This escalates the problem further.

Response: Sally's mother was an alcoholic. Sally knows her filtering system is strongly anti-alcohol, but she also recognizes that in our society kids are apt to experiment with alcohol. She lets herself feel her aversion to alcohol and her fear of it, sets it aside, steps back and reviews what will serve her kids best. She educates herself and them about alcohol and alcoholism, and gives them as much information as they need to make responsible choices for themselves. She detaches herself so that they can lead their lives and she can lead hers. The subject of alcohol is not particularly charged, one way or another, for her kids. When one of her children begins to manifest symptoms of alcoholism, he is able to recognize it and get help.

To be responsive is to be spontaneous, and by spontaneous I don't mean impulsive. The two words are sometimes used interchangeably, but impulsiveness comes out of reaction and spontaneity comes out of response.

Initially, it is difficult to tell when we're in reaction. It feels so much like "the way we are." As we observe ourselves, however, it becomes easier. We begin to notice that we're feeling out of control, helpless, or compelled to act in certain ways. The moment we recognize our reactions for what they are, we have moved from the past into the present. The Robot is on hold. We have become aware of what's going on. We have moved from being on automatic, where there is no choice, to being in observation, where we have a choice about what we are going to do next.

WHAT HAPPENS WHEN WE REACT

Many, many things happen to us, to the people around us, and to our communication when we react rather than respond. They aren't bad things; they just don't work particularly well. They don't produce the results of satisfying communication. Here's what happens when we react.

Communication stops dead.

Communication is the duplication of experience. When you are in reaction, you aren't experiencing anything and are thus giving the other person no experience to duplicate, even if he were prepared to do so.

When I was drinking alcohol I felt totally misunderstood by everyone, particularly my parents. Looking back, I can now see that I never communicated my experience—because I wasn't in touch with it. I cried, I complained, I made suicide attempts, I sulked. But, amazingly enough all of that was an *escape* from my true experience of bewilderment, helplessness, loss of control, fear, and feeling that I had let down everyone important to me. If I could have communicated that experience instead of my blame and rage, my parents could have much more easily helped me. At the same time, even if they could have heard my experience through that morass, I'm not sure I would ever have known it. My reactions were so rampant and strong, there was no way I could duplicate the fears, doubts, and helplessness they were feeling. I was creating too much interference. And of course, I've done the same as a parent. Regardless of how many communication seminars I've led, my first reaction when my children go into a state of hysteria or a major sulk is to want to shut them out. Fortunately, I no longer have to act on this reaction.

So, when you are in reaction, you can't hear the other person's experience. You're stuck behind your filters, and they are too thick for the other person's experience to penetrate. Most likely, neither of you is very interested in connecting with the other, anyhow. Do you like being close to someone who is caught in their file cabinet? No one does. There's nobody to connect with.

One of you is going to have to move into response in order for communication to take place, and if you wait for the other person, not only are the odds against his doing anything, but your abdication of the responsibility would take away all the fun.

Other people get sucked into your reaction
and start reacting themselves.
It's very hard to stay in present time when you're confronted with someone who has subconsciously substituted you for their first grade teacher or their mean old uncle, and who is reacting to you completely out of past pictures. You'll feel them doing this and your first impulse may be to go into reaction, too. If it's difficult for you to stay out of reaction now that you are aware of reactions and filters, then just think how hard it would be for someone who doesn't have that information.

In this way, an escalating chain reaction begins, and before you know it, the situation is completely out of control:

Your son has gone into his room and slammed the door in the middle of your objective and controlled explanation of why he can't go to the beer bust at the beach in your new Mercedes. You are determined to remain under control, but in reality you've lost it. You're fuming and you feel justified (always a danger sign).

He is now determined to make you react—because as soon as he does, he's won and you both know it. His every move is now designed to get your goat. He knows just how long to stay in his room, just when to come out "to get a coke." He knows just what facial expression to adopt, and it feels like he's doing it all on purpose. He's not. He's in reaction to your reaction, and you're in reaction to his.

At this point your best bet is to get in touch with the Observer. Your reactions will undoubtedly still be there, but at least you can watch them, which is the first step to self control. There are ways to deal with escalating reactions, and we will explore them later in this chapter, but why create the situation in the first place if it's possible not to?

You become a Robot.

The Mind is supposed to be our servant, not our master. But until we move out of reaction and back into response, we are the slaves of our Minds.

Watch someone who's in reaction. He or she is an automaton. The sole motivation is survival, a desperate drive to be right. That isn't indicative of who that person really is. The only thing that's happened is that they've forgotten that they are the choosers of their experience, and they've given all their power to their Minds.

Resistance creates persistence.

What you resist, will persist. I think of this as a law of the universe, just like water being wet and rocks being hard. It happens every time.

Here is how the resistance/persistence principle works. If we have certain filters that we'd rather not have because we think we're really superior to all that, then we are apt to deny them. The minute we deny them, we give them energy. Denial takes energy. Every time we try to suppress a thought or feeling, we simply concentrate energy on it. In this way we actually seem to double, triple, or quadruple the power we give to those thoughts or feelings.

If we resist, say, having fights with people in our family,

then our lives become centered around avoiding fights with those people. With all our energy concentrated in this area, unfortunately one fight after another breaks out. We are then likely to react by getting into the fight, tooth and nail, or by sticking our head in the sand while the world crumbles around us.

We can often tell what we're resisting in ourselves by checking out what we don't like about other people. If we can't stand people who are negative, it might be a good idea to look and see what we are resisting. This is especially true if we have a lot of people in our lives who all seem negative and we believe we are the one bright positive light. The universe and the Observer are trying to tell us something. We may have stuffed that thing we don't like about ourselves down pretty far, but we're being handed a road map to get to it—the reactions of other people.

Another clue to what we're resisting is that when the "forbidden" subject comes up, we're likely to go "unconscious:" We don't hear what's being said; we forget what was on the last page we read; we daydream, or in some way blank out our minds. If I'm feeling guilty about giving into my kid and letting him go to the beer bust on Saturday night, I don't really relish seeing articles in the morning paper about permissive parents and what damage they do to their children. I'll be so "unconscious," it'll take me five hours to read two paragraphs.

That's not my last chance, of course. The issue will come around again and again until I deal with my guilt. If the phone rings, and I think finally I have an excuse to get away from that newspaper article, it'll probably be my friend Sharon telling me about the kid who died in a DWI incident after a beer bust in Chicago.

Reaction leads to taking positions.

By taking a position, I mean sticking to a viewpoint relative to an issue or to another person.

Suppose I take the position that my husband is an alcoholic and alcoholics are irresponsible, weak people. As long as I hold that position, then no matter what I do, no matter how much I talk to him, or take him to AA meetings, or pour his booze down the sink, he remains a weak, irresponsible alcoholic. We're trapped in our positions on the board.

My life becomes concerned with trying to change him, fix him, and make him change his position. I can't see why he won't move. So much of my attention is focused on him, that I neglect to notice that I'm stuck in a position, too. The only way these positions can unlock is if one of us moves. If I wait for him, I could wait forever. If I really want to change the relationship, then I have to be the one to change it.

A good place to start might be to see what I'm getting out of this situation. There must be something, because I've kept it around for quite a while and put a great deal of energy into it. Maybe, as the nonalcoholic, I feel superior. Maybe I've never had much self-esteem, but next to him, I can feel terrific. If I can see what I'm getting out of the relationship the way it is, it will be easier for me to change my position. The next step is to see if I'm really willing to change it.

That's an important question: "Am I really willing to have this relationship change?" I don't want to answer automatically, because I may not be. I may be getting more out of it the way it is than I'm willing to give up. One thing is certain, if I alter my position, he will alter, too. I'm going to have an entirely different situation on my hands.

How do you tell if you're in a position? If the relationship is staying the same, one or both of you are in a position about the other one or about the relationship. It doesn't matter whether he's in it or you're in it. The only way you're going to change it is to leave your position. You're not going to be able to force him from his. You have to move first.

The people in "Tough Love" are helping each other do just

that. Tough Love is an organization of parents who support one another in getting out of their old positions of permissiveness and taking a stand that is tougher. These parents loved their kids but often found it difficult to set standards and to have their kids abide by those standards. That may look like they had no position, but in fact, they had the position of having *no* position. Now they're taking responsibility for the situation, not by taking responsibility away from the kids, but by giving the kids the responsibility for abiding by the standards.

A lot of those people probably had taken the position that they wanted to be better parents than their parents were. So they set out to be "perfect parents," but they weren't producing the results that they wanted. Their kids were a mess. When they moved from the position of having to be perfect parents, the kids started moving from the position of proving that their parents weren't perfect. The kids might not have liked it, but they moved.

I don't mean that everything will transform itself overnight. When you first change a position, nobody knows how to be or what to do. You have to live with it for a while and keep focused on the results you want to produce. If you stay with it, commit yourself and be responsible for it, then it will work.

A client of mine, Merita, had a "no-good" daughter who was heavily involved in punk rock and cocaine, and had green hair and failing grades in school. The day Merita changed her position about her daughter was the day she realized she had a stake in keeping her "no good." Merita needed to prove that her ex-husband was at fault for deserting them when their daughter was a baby. Merita saw that she had a choice—either to be right about the devastating impact of her husband's desertion, or for her daughter to have a happy life. It was not an easy choice to make. If she chose the latter it meant giving up years of resentment which had served as an energy source, and it meant accepting some true responsibility for her daughter's well-being. But she did choose it.

There were no immediate miracles. If anything, her daughter outwardly hated the new restrictions on her hair color and her freedom to come and go as she pleased. In time, however, Merita and her daughter began to respect each other. The transformation of the relationship was under way.

RESPONDING TO
OUR OWN REACTIONS

We aren't going to stop reacting, anymore than we're going to stop judging, deciding, or filtering. What we want to be able to do in order to get back in control and stop behaving like a panel of buttons just waiting to be pushed, is to be able to *respond to our reactions*.

That may sound a little strange and complicated at first, but it only means we let ourselves have whatever reaction we have, without compounding the reaction by saying, "OH! NO! I've done it again! I've reacted! Jumped right into the file cabinet. Oh, woe is me!" Or else, "Well I was justified. It was the right thing to do. There was nothing else I could have done!" Instead, we simply observe what reaction we had, step back, and say, "Okay, I had that reaction. Now what do I want to do about it?"

Say, for example, that for the tenth time this month your boss gives you an impossible deadline to meet. Your first reaction might be frustration and hopelessness, even anger. That's fine, but then you can step back and realize that being given tough deadlines reminds you of the endless chores you were given as a child that you never seemed to be able to finish. Then, instead of giving in to the feelings of hopelessness that have been restimulated, you can just acknowledge that they are there and keep on working without being controlled by your initial reaction.

In essence, responsibility is the ability to respond to our reactions. When we look at it that way, responsibility becomes a lot easier to take. It boils down to not giving ourselves such a hard time. It means letting ourselves react to situations and stimuli, and then stepping back and responding from the observer rather than jumping more deeply into our minds.

If we can learn to respond to our own reactions, it will be a lot easier to respond to other people's reactions. If we can't do it with ourselves, our chances of doing it with someone else are slim.

RESPONDING TO
OTHER PEOPLE'S REACTIONS

Sometimes people who are just beginning to work with responses and reactions think, "Gee, the world sure would be a better place if everyone were in response all the time. Then I wouldn't have to work so hard at responding to other people's reactions."

If you and I are in perfect communication, then there's really nothing to respond to. We're already there. To have a response, there must be something to reply to, a reaction to step out of. Response is a tool for moving out of reaction and into observation and choice.

"Response-ability," then, is the ability to respond in the midst of chaos, confusion, and upset. In other words, in the midst of reaction; more precisely, in the midst of our family.

Here's what happens if I react to someone else's reaction:

Suppose I'm a recovered alcoholic with nineteen years of sobriety, and my daughter is manifesting alcoholism. I'm so relieved when she finally comes to me to talk about it, and she feels safe because I'm her mother *and* a former alcoholic. She decides as a result of our conversation (to my delight) to stop drinking. I think, "This is just wonderful!" But the next thing I know, she's having delirium tremens (DTs—a strong physical and emotional withdrawal from alcohol often involving convulsions and hallucinations). I never had DTs, so I don't know what to do. I go into reaction to her DTs, which are of course *her* reaction. I panic and give her a drink. Now everything's fine, except the communication never fulfilled itself and we're both back right where we started. She's drinking again; neither of us believes she can get along without drinking and the whole thing's a mess.

My options in this case were: a) to get professional help, b) to grab her, hold her and talk to her, which is often what works with people having DTs. If I'd done that, we might both have had the strength to get through it and the communication would still be open. To make the communication work, I have to be willing to be uncomfortable—to be scared, to not know what to do. I have to be willing to keep responding in the face of the unknown.

We all say we want people to be honest and open with us, but the truth is, we want it on our terms. We want it unless it presses our "buttons" for feeling angry, afraid, inferior, etc. If we want true communication, we have to be willing to get our buttons pressed and still keep responding.

Most communication takes place at the level of everybody's reaction to everybody else. True communication is a matter of watching our reactions to their reactions, and staying detached enough to pull out of the reaction once the feeling is experienced. Then we can make whatever response we choose to make in the present moment, rather than reacting blindly based on the past and on our own particular filters.

In the end, we are the observers and choosers of our own experience. We can choose what we're going to do with our reactions. We can stay in them or we can step out of them.

Communication is a process that's always developing, always changing and growing in the present moment. The duplication of experience goes beyond understanding. It is never the same from minute to minute.

When we have the ability to respond to our own reactions and to the reactions of others, we can forget about blame and guilt and simply respond to whatever the current situation is. The more responsible we become, the more spontaneous we can be. The freedom to communicate spontaneously comes directly out of our ability to "answer to" the present.

KIDS ARE GOING TO REACT.
COUNT ON IT!

We're not talking about *if* your children react; we're talking about *when* they react. Kids are great at reaction, and teenagers are the world champions. Not only are they going to react, they're going to react differently from us and differently from one another. There's no way you can count on or predict anything about their reactions. You have to be on your toes all the time.

Research increasingly indicates that children come into the world with clear and different personality traits. Some people believe that children react individually from the moment of conception. It has certainly been established that although the fetus in the womb may not be able to formulate conscious or rational thoughts, it does have reactions which differ strikingly from one individual to the other. Hospital nurses have long observed that babies react differently from one another from birth. Thus, it appears that the environment plays less of a role than was once thought. Regardless of the child's position in the family or what the parents did or didn't do, many of his patterns of behavior are set from the time he is very small, perhaps before the parents have had a chance to interact with him at all.

I think parents sometimes get the idea that it's their job to take this little piece of clay and mold it into a genius, or a great athlete, or the perfectly behaved child. But growing up just doesn't work that way, as most parents ultimately find out—sometimes the hard way. Parents can create certain kids of environments and provide certain things for their children, but eventually the children have to pursue their own lives. In the end, they become what they are and not what their parents make them.

We're so concerned about the impact that parents have on children that we forget to look at something that's just as important: the impact that children have on parents.

YOU'RE HUMAN, TOO

Somehow, we get the notion that because parents are older and more experienced than children, they're supposed to do everything right and that if something is wrong, it's the parents' fault. That assumption forms the basis for a lot of problems between parents and children.

Where did we get the idea that we have to be perfect parents? Have you ever met one? Does the species even exist? By the very act of putting ourselves in that role of "perfect parent," we create a problem—both for ourselves and for our children. We're assuming a role, a disguise. Kids can't stand disguises, especially in their parents. It reminds them too much of their own pretenses, which they're having a terrible time trying to get into place.

Some people think that if they are good parents, they will never let their Robots react. Good luck! There isn't a person alive who doesn't go into reaction, and the primary thing some parents react to is the idea of not being good parents. That in itself will set them up not to be good parents, no matter how good they look on the surface. Resistance creates persistence.

The truth is that all any of us can do is the best we know how. In fact, that's what all of us do. Even the people who beat their children are doing the best they know how. They're attempting to get control of the situation. When the kids start screaming the parents feel powerless, out of control, exhausted. They don't know what to do, and based on decisions they've made as children, they react.

Many child abusers were abused themselves. When they were little and they were beaten, they felt powerless. The person who had the power was the parent who was beating them. So they made the decision that, "If I want to have power, then I have to beat someone." With such a decision operating, someone is going to get hurt—usually the child. The parent needs help, not condemnation.

The point is to acknowledge that, whatever kind of job you think you're doing as a parent, *you're doing the best you know how to do.* There is no such thing as the perfect parent, and you can only get into trouble trying to be one. Let yourself be however you are. This gives you the opportunity to become a more responsive parent—which is what you're really after anyway.

DON'T TAKE IT PERSONALLY

The same goes for your kids. You have to let them be however they are, as imperfect as that may sometimes seem to you. As I said earlier, we're not saying here that children should have the freedom to create havoc and destruction in the world. But they do have a right to be themselves, no matter how much you nag them and no matter how bad they may look to you. Children are growing, developing human beings, and they will do strange things—things that will make us miserable if we take them personally. We can almost count on our children manifesting whatever behaviors we've decided aren't all right. Most likely, they will be the ones we think will reflect on us as parents.

Tom, for instance, thinks it's all right if his son Tommy, seven, gets into fights with other little boys. He doesn't encourage it, but he figures it's part of life and something Tommy will grow out of. He doesn't make a big deal of it when Tommy comes home a little scratched up. Very soon, Tommy loses interest in fighting. It's not fun, it gives you bruises, and besides, you don't get much of a reaction from your father by doing it.

Wetting the bed, on the other hand, is something that Tom, Sr. can't deal with. He thinks it's just about the most shameful thing that could happen. If Tommy wets the bed, Tom lets him know how awful it is in no uncertain terms. The result is that Tommy's bedwetting persists—and persists; Tom Sr. is so ashamed of the problem he won't even take Tommy to the doctor for the medical help he may need.

Tom's reactions didn't have to do with Tommy so much as they had to do with himself. Somehow, it didn't reflect badly on him as a parent if Tommy got into fights, but it did if Tommy wet his bed. Naturally, what he resisted is what he got.

The situation that just kills some parents is the two-year-old who runs around the house all day screaming, "I hate you!" at the top of its lungs. Kids love it, but it really upsets the parents if they don't know that this is normal for children of that age. They don't expect it, and worse, they believe it. They take it personally. The more they resist it, of course, the louder the kids scream.

The important thing to remember is that, whatever our children do, it's not personal. If we can think of our children as being "on loan" rather than as our possessions, it's much easier to keep our perspective. The next time you go into reaction over your child's decision to leave the church and join the Moonies, or to join the political party most in opposition to yours, pretend that he is your neighbor's child. You may be amazed at your ability to respond in a way that sets an example for children to follow.

DETACHMENT, NOT DESERTION

In order not to take our children's words and actions personally, we need to be able to detach. Most people are afraid to detach from their children because they think it means they're deserting them. Detachment doesn't mean that at all. It simply means that you separate your identity, your survival, and your values from your children's development. That's the furthest thing in the world from desertion. It lets you be closer to them, more aware of what their experience is, and more supportive than perhaps you've ever been before.

Detaching means allowing our children to have their own lives, whether we like how they look or not. That doesn't mean that we withdraw our love and support from them. We stay close enough to hear them, so we can duplicate their experience and respond to it, but not so close that our vision is distorted. If we can duplicate their experience, then they are free and we are free. And finally, we can begin to communicate.

Simple examples of detaching are knowing that your worth as a homemaker isn't tied up in your child's clean room, or your masculinity isn't tied up in having your son make the soccer team. However, when your child is involved in alcohol or other drugs, things can get more complicated. Perhaps you fear for your child's health—or even for his life. In this situation detaching seems much easier said than done. But it is all the more essential if any change is to take place.

Detaching in a life-threatening situation absolutely requires getting support for *yourself*. Otherwise there is little chance that you will remain detached in times of crisis. And crisis of some kind is often necessary before an addicted child can recover.

As a parent, I know it is difficult to remain detached when your child is not doing well in school, seems to have lost motivation, is depressed, or is acting out in destructive ways. Our feelings range from guilt, to anger, to fear, to despair and a sense of inadequacy. We just know if we could find the right answer our child would change.

The day a friend of mine decided not to bail her son out of jail for a DWI arrest was the turning point in their relationship and in his life. For the first time, he realized he could no longer manipulate her into rescuing him. But her detachment did not mean she felt indifferent. If anything, her sorrow, and guilt initially were greater than they had ever been. Her feelings for him, no longer covered up with the rescuer's resentment, were difficult to bear. Nonetheless, she carried it through, and the results were worth it.

Detachment means getting the message that we can't change our child. We can only change ourselves. The miracle is that by so doing, we finally give our children the opportunity to change themselves.

TO BE HEARD, "EMPTY THE SPACE"

Before anything else can happen, we have to be willing to hear our children's experience. If we try to get any information over to them without first finding out where they are and giving them a chance to let go of it, we just simply aren't going to get our information across, let alone have them duplicate our experience.

So before we can be heard, we have to "empty the space." We do this by being willing to hear them first. It's like emptying a coffee cup before trying to pour any more coffee into it.

When I go into elementary school classrooms to talk about alcoholism, the kids' minds are filled with all kinds of misconceptions and misinformation about alcohol and alcoholism. I have to find out what their ideas are and give them a chance to "empty them out" if I'm to have any chance of being heard. I think their misconceptions are attitudes, but the kids think they're the truth. If I don't let them express them, they'll be holding on to them for dear life and won't hear a thing I say.

The same holds true with my own children. If I'm unwilling to hear their viewpoints on the relative safety of marijuana, if I go berserk the moment the subject comes up, there's no opportunity for them to express their viewpoint, so they're stuck with it. Hearing them makes it possible for them to move into a new idea. It also teaches them how to hear you, which means that you can begin to move more readily also!

Don't, however, get the idea that you must always listen to and hear everything your children say, because it's wrong not to. That's not giving yourself permission to be human. There will be many times when, if the truth be known, you're simply not willing to listen. The worst thing you can do in that case is fake it. If you're in reaction and mad as hell, then it isn't going to work to sit there icily and pretend you're responding just because you're being quiet, rather than screaming. Everyone will know how you feel, and your anger will scare them to death.

Remember, kids are capable of playing the same game. If you see that expression that says, "Who, me? Reacting? Just look how calm I am!" then take another look. You're probably dealing with a raging reaction.

If you react from time to time, so what? The only important thing is to tell the truth when you're reacting, rather than trying to pretend you're responding. You don't have to justify or rationalize your reaction. It's just something you did because you're a human being.

ESCALATING REACTIONS AND HOW TO DEAL WITH THEM

The way Alice and her mother, Karen, have set up an exchange of reactions is that Alice is wrong for smoking pot and Karen is right for trying to make her stop. In the past, Alice could pretty much count on the fact that if she showed up for breakfast with red, glassy eyes, then Karen would yell at her, "Alice, have you been smoking pot again? I told you to stop that!" It was a predictable reaction. All Alice had to do was press the button, and those words would come out. It happened every time.

Then one morning, Alice showed up for breakfast with red, glassy eyes and Karen didn't react. No words, no screaming. The pattern had been broken. Alice found this lack of reaction confusing and even mildly upsetting. Her predictable world wasn't quite so predictable anymore. What does she do? The only thing she can do is to try and get her world back to normal, so she escalates her reaction. She comes home with very red, very glassy eyes *and* alcohol on her breath. Still no reaction. Now Alice is really upset, and will do almost anything to get Karen to scream at her. She can't make it happen, though, and eventually bursts into tears. Chances are good that now Karen and Alice can at least talk.

Still, Alice may continue to escalate her reaction in some way. All Karen can do is to keep responding and communicating. She can perceive Alice's state of being again and again if necessary, and communicate again that she doesn't want to play the "red, glassy eyes/screaming," right/wrong game anymore.

Sooner or later, Alice will get the message. Karen will have changed their relationship from reaction to response.

Needless to say, this changing takes lots of patience, with yourself and with your kids. It means continuing to respond in the face of reaction, on top of reaction, on top of reaction. And that responding may take different forms from what either you or your kids think it should.

Maybe your kid is one of those who gets terrible cookie cravings an hour before dinner, and he's just asked for the thirty-second time, "MMoooommmmmm, can I have a cookie? Just one." Your normal reaction may be to say calmly and cooly, as the perfect parent, "No, Charlie, it'll spoil your dinner." Your true response might be to scream, "If you ask me that one more time, I'm going to explode!" and kick him out of the kitchen.

Your yelling may shock him a little, but it may also intrigue him and make him feel relieved. If it's an honest response, it'll probably feel better to him than the cool buttoned-down reaction he's used to getting.

There is only one rule concerning responding: Never use physical violence of any kind. Now you may say, "Wait a minute, Karen is supposed to respond and not yell at Alice, yet it's all right to yell at the cookie whiner. What's going on here?"

What's going on here is this: It's neither right nor wrong to yell. There are times when yelling is a response, there are times when it is a reaction. Karen's yelling was constant and predictable. Therefore it could be used by Alice as a manipulative device. Karen needed to look at it, see if it was working, and choose. In the second example, we are assuming that your "normal" reaction is to speak calmly and coolly. That is as much a reaction as yelling, because alternatives are not available. So, true communication takes place at the level of alternatives—almost boundless ones.

You may be noticing a recurring theme: to stop worrying so much about what we should be doing to or for our children and to pay more attention to our own reactions and processes. If fact, to be honest with ourselves, to live our lives according to our own lights, and to become more and more of ourselves is the best—and the only—thing we can really do for our children.

LEAVING VERSUS COMMITMENT

Sometimes it all sounds too hard. When it looks like communication is never going to work, you want to leave—literally or figuratively.

It's not that you don't want to learn, to grow, to enrich your relationships, but surely at some other time, in some other place, with some other people, the whole thing would be a lot easier. That's what the Mind says, anyway, and that's when the tricky subject of commitment begins to rear its head.

Being committed to a relationship means that you've *chosen* to stay with it even if it gets uncomfortable or difficult. It means that you aren't going to turn around and run off at the first hint of trouble.

Most people don't even conceive of the parent-child relationship as one that can be run from (although it actually happens, either physically or emotionally, more often than we'd like to admit). Most people wouldn't consciously leave their children, no matter how bad the relationship becomes. But as strong as this blind belief in the parent-child bond can be, it excludes an even more powerful bond: commitment by choice. For even in the parent-child relationship, we do have a choice. Without that choice, there can't be any commitment to the individual child. You may merely be trapped.

Even if it sounds sacrilegious to you, you might sit down sometime and really think about whether you want to be in a relationship with your children. This is frightening because it opens possibilities that most of us consider scandalous. What if you discovered that you actually didn't like them or want to live with them?

There are times—and we'll discuss them further on—when it is better to give the care and management of your children to people who are better able to handle them. If you truly don't want your children, you probably should be considering some alternatives. To be with our children solely because it is the "right," "expected," or legal obligation is to strike a death knell to the relationship.

One of the happiest people I know is a woman who was raised by her grandmother. Her mother came to visit on occasion, but not very often. This woman knew her mother gave her up out of love because she just wasn't emotionally suited to raising a child. Believe me, if you and your child despise each other, the only way you'll get past it is to give each other the option of a different environment.

One woman I know loves to be with her grown daughter— for no more than three hours at any one time. Because they have learned not to take each other's idosyncrasies personally, they now have a superb relationship and wonderful times together, but never for more than a three-hour stretch!

If you sit down and really look at it, however, you'll probably find that you do want to be in a committed relationship with your children. Just having taken the time and the risk to make that choice will begin to enrich your relationship. You're not together because you *have* to be; you're together because you *want* to be.

Let's say you've done that: you've consciously chosen to commit to your children. Of course, the first thing that happens is some terrible upset. You'll probably want to go right back and reevaluate the whole thing. Maybe you aren't strong enough just now. Guess where all those thoughts and voices are coming from. Your Mind is at it again, trying to protect you from experience and from the unknown.

At this point, you'll value your ability to identify your Mind talking and to detach from it. Then you can return to your commitment and continue responding as much as you can, putting one foot in front of the other and trusting that the communication is going to open up.

Human beings want more than anything else to be connected to other people. We want to respond to others and be responded to. When you stay with your commitment to communication, you're going with the way of nature and you can't lose.

FIVE

Parents' Attitudes
Meet Kids' Attitudes.
Look Out!

PARENTS' ATTITUDES:
WHAT THEY ARE, WHERE THEY
COME FROM, WHAT THEY DO

An attitude is a disposition to act in a certain way that is grounded in feeling or opinion and expressed through manners, postures, or positions. Attitudes are part of the filter system through which we see the world, and they reflect decisions we've made (based in the past) about the way things were, or the way things *should be*. What is more, we often have attitudes about attitudes. Interestingly these are apt to be remarkably similar to the attitudes themselves. We hate people who are hateful. We judge people who are judgmental. Our attitudes are reflected back and forth, from one person to another. And because we inevitably draw to us the attitudes that we condemn most, we are very likely to find those attitudes in our children—and they are likely to find their least favorite attitudes in us.

If we think we have an attitude that's negative or unattractive, we will try to cover it up with a positive attitude. Of course our kids are the first to know it, and they don't like it, either. Their reaction? They'll turn right around and manifest or act out the negative attitude we don't want to face.

Perhaps I've decided conceited people are bad, and so I try to be very humble. That way, I'm better than all those dreadful people out there who are conceited (which, of course, means I'm conceited). The next thing I know, my kid is telling everyone how great he is, bragging and acting conceited. I can't stand it. Not only can't I stand having someone around me who's conceited and constantly reminding me of my fears about myself, but now I've got a kid who doesn't look any better than the other kids. In fact, he looks worse. That makes me look terrible indeed! And the whole point of covering up the conceit was to look better! The whole mess is compounded by the fact that seldom is any of this done consciously.

What we try to do by "improving" our attitudes is to make ourselves better people and to make our kids better people, but very often the results we produce are just a lot of conflict and pain. As with other filters, if we try to deny our attitudes, we get stuck with them forever. If we recognize them, we can bring them into the light and choose whether we want to keep them around or not.

I don't want to suggest that we should obsessively try to weed out every little attitude. It's much more fun to view the process as an adventure, a stimulating and revitalizing opportunity to develop self-awareness and really satisfying relationships with our kids. Unearthing all these parts of ourselves is a little like going on a treasure hunt.

Let's say, for example, that you have a child who is an overeater. To you this represents an attitude of not caring about his body, and that makes you angry. You may think that you're doing everything you possibly can to care for your body. You eat nothing but health foods, jog twice a day and drink wheat grass juice. If his overeating angers you, though, there's more going on here than meets the eye.

It may be that all the things you do for your body come out of righteousness. You think you *should* take care of it, and bend over backward to prove you're doing so, but it's an unconscious protective scheme to hide the fact that you don't really care about your body. The jogging, the healthy eating, and the wheat grass juice are just a set of rules, someone else's good ideas about what you should do if you care about your body. But you whip that poor body into shape just to prove (to yourself as much as to others) that you don't have a bad attitude.

Meanwhile, every time your kid reaches for a candy bar, he knows the reaction that his action produces. I don't mean to imply that he's being Machiavellian. It's just the normal thing for him to do. It gets him a lot of attention.

So what do you do now? How do you defuse this situation in which your child overeats and you react because you don't really care about your body? The first thing, of course, is to tell the truth. Do you really want to take care of your body, or are you just doing it because you think you should?

Maybe you don't really want to exercise or maybe it would be fine if you just didn't have to drink the wheat grass juice anymore. When you face the truth, it may turn out to be, "I don't really want to do all those extreme things. I just want to do a little exercise and eat healthy foods. But no wheat grass juice. I'm not crazy about exercising, but I want the results I get from it, so I'll do it."

You have to be careful, though, about being righteous if you choose to go ahead and do something that produces the result you want, even if you're not happy about what you have to do to get there. There's a tendency to turn around and say, "I'm willing to do what's good for me, kid. Why aren't you?" That, as you can imagine, could start a real incident.

INTENTION
AND ATTITUDE

Let's go back to the example of the kid eating candy bars. Why is he still doing it? Why hasn't the message gotten across? Perhaps intention is preventing it.

We said earlier that being responsible for your intention means taking the point of view that people receive exactly the communication we intend for them to receive. Somehow, I must not want my kid to get the message and stop eating those candy bars!

This is touchy; few people want to hear it. Sometimes it's possible for our own self-esteem to be so low that we're threatened by our kids. Maybe we don't really want our kids to have their acts together, because we don't have ours together. Most parents would deny this and say, "Oh, no. I really want my child to be a success."

But look at the results. Is the kid a success? Whatever you see out there is what the true intention is. Maybe I'd just as soon my kid threw some sugar in his body, if I'm not too thrilled about my own. I sure don't want a potential Arnold Schwarzenegger or Bo Derek lurking around my house watching my stomach protrude or my thighs getting fat.

I've worked with many children (of all ages) who have said things such as, "I can't earn more money than my Dad," or "I can't be thinner than my Mom." Some kids, of course, do make more money than their dads and are thinner than their moms, but very often they don't get any satisfaction from it. They feel too guilty.

I don't mean to imply that kids have no control over their own destiny. Ultimately *they choose* what they will make of their lives and what they will turn out to be. But we do have an impact on them with our attitudes and our communication, and the options available to them will be greater if their choices are not limited by the need to make us either right or wrong.

WHY ATTITUDES
ARE SO POWERFUL

An attitude is a mainstay, or, as the dictionary says, an orientation. It gives direction and tells us where we are. Everything else falls into place relative to the attitude.

We choose attitudes based either on protection or expansion. Any attitude you're attached to, defensive about, or need to justify or rationalize, stems from the need to be right. Attitudes chosen to support your expansion do not need to be defended or explained. They were chosen to serve, and will be kept only as long as they serve. We are not those attitudes, and we don't need them to survive.

PARENTS' ATTITUDES
MEET KIDS' ATTITUDES

Frankenstein meets Godzilla? Sometimes it seems that way.

Attitudes aren't something one acquires at puberty or at the age of twenty-one. Children are just as capable of having attitudes as their parents are. They may even have more of them, and it's absolutely certain that they go through them faster.

Kids try on attitudes, thoughts, and behaviors the same way they try on clothes. They don't buy everything they try on. They're just experimenting with new ways of thinking and behaving, and learning that life presents them with many options.

"Of course," we say—until something they try on runs smack into one of our protectionist attitudes. If I have a filter that says children must get straight A's in school or they won't succeed in life, the chances are very good that I will end up with a child who gets terrible grades in school. He'll probably be smart, too; he just won't care. That'll distress me even more than if I thought he wasn't so bright and *couldn't* get good grades.

The problem is not that he is getting terrible grades; the problem is that my filter says he can't succeed unless he gets good grades. He's either going to swallow that belief or try to make me very wrong.

If I can recognize the attitude and start to let go of the fear that caused me to adopt it in the first place, then I can begin to look at the real issue, which is that my kid simply isn't getting good grades. From there, I may be able to detach enough to support him in actually getting better grades, or to support him in being a success despite the fact that he doesn't get good grades.

In other words, I need to simplify matters by getting down to the real issue. The first step is to unhook the issue of the grades from the issue of my feelings about not being a success. That may involve being willing to experience my own feelings of insecurity, inferiority, fear, sadness, or whatever I think comes with not being a success.

Our beliefs and attitudes can create their own reality around them. If I have an attitude that addicts or alcoholics are failures, and my child starts to have trouble with alcohol, then I may make the equation that he is now going to be a failure. If I do that, I may just encourage my child to be both an alcoholic and a failure, rather than simply dealing with the issue that he is starting to have a problem with alcohol.

PROLIFERATING MONSTER ATTITUDES

We can count on the fact that our kids are going to pick up and try on a lot of different attitudes, and that they will select chiefly those that push our "buttons." They will come up with opinions that are the antithesis of what we believe. They're going to seem narrow, adamant, and opinionated to us.

It's difficult, as parents, to look at a kid who really hasn't experienced much of life and to hear him spouting ludicrous theories and philosophies. He's saying we should all be Communists or Socialists, whereas we fought in Vietnam. Or he thinks our favorite political candidate is a joke. But what does he know?

Kids come up with the most outrageous ideas in the areas of religion and life-style, and they treat you as though you were an absolute nerd for believing anything different and for living the way you live. Our first instinct is to make them stop. We think, "This isn't appropriate. It isn't right. It isn't respectful." We think if they keep talking like that, they're going to get into all kinds of terrible trouble. We start thinking about the SLA, the Chicago Seven, Kent State, the cults, the Moonies, LSD, PCP, the drug underworld, and all the other things they could get into.

Difficult as all this is, it's also the most natural thing in the world. This is how people grow up. We grew up by disagreeing with our parents. Disagreement isn't something we want to discourage. But I certainly don't recommend going *into* agreement with them, and saying, "Why yes, the SLA sounds like a wonderful idea!" I am suggesting, however, that we listen carefully and try to get behind the words to hear what their message really is.

Your child may announce, for instance, that LSD is the key to enlightenment. If all we hear is "LSD," and we become crazed with anxiety, we'll never be able to hear what they're really talking about. They're probably talking more about enlightenment than about LSD, and more about new, exciting perspectives than about enlightenment.

We have to be willing to get beyond what they seem to be saying on the surface, and to do this before we burst out in a tirade and punish them. We need to get to the point where we can duplicate what they're experiencing. If we can do that, and they know we have done it, they'll be a lot more willing to try and experience our viewpoints. When there is a conflict, they may be more willing to listen to what we have to say. That may not happen right away, but sooner or later they'll begin to see that since we're willing to listen to them, it's not so dangerous for them to listen to us.

In their early years, they largely took the world as we presented it to them. Now they're learning about new things, seeing the world in a new light and thinking, "Maybe I don't exactly agree with what my parents said." If we don't allow them to have all those wild thoughts when they arise, if we fight and resist them, they'll be trapped there and we'll have those thoughts around us forever. Teens may hold on even more strongly than adults because at this point their positions are a bit more vulnerable and unstable, and they know it. For our own sakes, it's best to let them be—so they can move on.

It's the same old story. Whatever we resist will persist. Whatever we can't or won't accept in ourselves or someone else will come back to haunt us again and again.

TAKING A STAND

When we talk about letting kids be the way they are, we obviously don't mean letting them do things that put them in severe danger—physically, emotionally, mentally, spiritually. We don't mean letting them do things that put *us* in that kind of danger, either, or things that we don't want done in our homes. We are the parents, after all. It's our house and we do get to vote.

If there's something you consider very important—either to you or to your child—you have the right to make that opinion known and even to make a rule about it. If you don't want swearing in your house, for instance, you can take a stand. If you do that, though, you have to be willing to follow through on it.

My suggestion is to have very few rules, and to enforce them thoroughly and consistently. The fewer rules you can get by with, the better. Then you can stick to your guns, say, "This is the way I want it," and make it that way.

There is one thing we know about rules. If our kids' spiritual upbringing is terribly important to us, and whether they drink and take other drugs is terribly important, and whether they have sex is terribly important, and whether they put away the dishes is terribly important, and whether they take out the garbage is terribly important, and whether being a Republican or Democrat is terribly important, then very soon we have too many rules and really can't draw any lines.

They don't know what's *really* important, and neither do we. We can't give them any true guidance. We become nagging machines. Even if we say nothing and just look dissatisfied and disapproving, they'll get the message and it'll have the same effect that all the screaming did, or worse.

They'll completely tune out. "It's just another one of Mom or Dad's things," they'll think. And they'll be right. We'll have lost our boundaries and our values, trying to impose an impossible set of standards on them so that we can look like perfect parents. The results will be that no one is happy and we are anything but perfect parents.

How do you know what rules to set and which to let go? Well, you don't. You just have to follow your instincts and know that it's going to turn out however it turns out and that you've done your best.

Let's say we think that our child's spiritual or religious wellbeing is the most important thing, so one of our rules is that he goes to church every Sunday. It could turn out that the kid learns to go to church as a habit, appreciates what we taught him, and does it for the rest of his life. Or it could turn out that he turns against the church completely and won't have anything to do with it ever again. It could turn out that he decides to have nothing to do with the church for twenty years, and then goes back to it and is grateful for his early training. We don't know what the results are going to be. All we can do is what we feel is best today, in the present moment.

I personally draw the line at what I consider issues of physical, emotional, or spiritual survival. There are certain things that are absolutely not allowed when it comes to alcohol and other drugs, such as drinking and driving. I don't like messy rooms, but I'm a lot less concerned about them or whether the dogs get fed on time than I am about whether my kid is drinking and driving, so that is where I lay down the law in my own household.

When it comes to experimenting with drugs, I want my children to be well-informed so that they know what the drugs are and what will happen to their bodies and minds if they take them. I don't take the point of view that alcohol and other drugs are bad, but rather the point of view that I'm interested in my children's health and well-being.

I don't lecture my children. I become thoroughly educated about touchy subjects and drop information in the form of casual comments, magazine articles, or pertinent pamphlets. And, because my children know that I'm interested in their health and well-being, they listen. They even read the articles—though they usually don't let me know it until months later.

Many parents say, "Well, thank God it's just alcohol!" if their children are drinking, but become apoplectic at the very mention of other drugs. In such an environment, the kids can't wait to get their hands on various substances and try them out.

Basically, we want to give our kids guidelines for their behavior without curbing their privilege to experience, to let them know what is acceptable and what is not without making anybody right or wrong.

Rules can also have the positive function of something kids can rebel against, something that they can oppose, in order to really develop their thinking and ability to deal with their world.

Your family might benefit by your taking a stand or an attitude with them, one that you realize you're not overly attached to, and then backing off it when they pressure you. Give them a chance to watch you let go of an attitude. Don't just pretend, though; watch yourself and see if you can move from that position. After you've heard them out, say, "Okay, you're right. I see what you mean. Let's do it your way." It's valuable for children to experience their own power, and to see that it doesn't destroy people to move out of a position. They also know that you're a big enough person to do just that.

THE GOALS OF PARENTHOOD

Most parents want basically the same things for their children. They want their children to grow up able to think, choose, and act for themselves. They want them to be able to take care of themselves and function independently in the world.

That's a big order in this day and age, because everything is moving fast and changing quickly. To have a child grow up to be physically, emotionally, and spiritually fulfilled in this world is something of a miracle. Sometimes people look at the younger generation and shake their heads, but I think it's amazing that kids turn out as well as they do, considering what they have to contend with.

Our children are living in a world that is utterly unlike the world in which we grew up. They're programming computers, breaking athletic records, living in the midst of an information and media explosion, and having levels of exposure to such things as sex, alcohol, and other drugs in their early teens that we had in our early twenties.

If ever a generation needed to know how to think, choose, and act for themselves moment to moment, it's this generation. Whereas we needed to learn information, they need to learn how to learn. The old attitudes and paradigms and filters—*our* attitudes and paradigms and filters—won't work anymore. Nor will it work to shift from old filters and attitudes to new ones. *Any* filter will keep them stuck, immobile—and that is something our children's world won't tolerate. We want our children to be able to keep up with the times, to stay on top of things and not be engulfed by their world.

We have to free our minds and allow them to free their minds so that they can progress at the rate at which things are happening. We have to let them become "centered" in their ability to deal with the world. We need to instill in them a desire to keep looking, to keep learning and responding, and not to get stuck.

When I say we want our children to be able to "think" for themselves, I mean we want them to be able to observe, to experience and to weigh matters. We want them to be able to go beyond thinking, actually, to see how things really are—to truly perceive a situation to the best of their ability regardless of what their own positions or points of view are.

When I say we want our children to be able to "act" for themselves, that also means allowing for the possibility of "not acting," if that is more appropriate. Your twelve-year-old daughter might, out of the goodness of her heart, want to keep her drunken uncle from hitting his wife, but it might not be appropriate for her to step in if she's just going to escalate the fight as well as get beaten in the process!

We want our children to act appropriately. When someone suggests that they buy a six-pack of beer and share it in the car, we want them to know that that's neither appropriate nor legal.

When I say we want our children to be able to "choose" for themselves, I mean we want them to be able to select freely among alternatives. I don't mean "decide," which is to murder alternatives in order to protect themselves from the unknown and survive by being right.

We want them to think, choose, and act not out of rebellion or coercion, but based on their individual responses to their world.

That can only happen to the extent that we don't impose our attitudes on them, and *there's the rub*.

We want the best for them, and those old attitudes worked for us. We have to keep reminding ourselves that imposing our attitudes on them only pushes our kids into a corner.

WHY WE IMPOSE OUR ATTITUDES ON OUR KIDS

We impose our attitudes on our children with the best of intentions. We want them, to profit from what we've learned, and not have to suffer some of the things we suffered and saw others suffer. But sometimes these very reasons become the obstacles to the goals we set out to achieve as parents. There are five basic things that can get in the way.

We want our children to avoid our mistakes.
We've seen what works and what doesn't work, and we want to pass on our knowledge to them. We know where all the potholes are in the road, and we don't want our kids stepping in them.

We want them to achieve what we've achieved.
We pulled ourselves up by our bootstraps and we made it, so that should work for them, too. We're married and we're happy, so all they have to do is get married and they'll be happy, too.

As we've already seen, this attitude usually backfires. We forget that whatever our "it" is isn't necessarily what everyone wants. We forget that our children might be happier and better off living in an entirely different kind of neighborhood than we did, earning less money, married to a completely different kind of person (or not married at all), not having any children, or living on the other side of the country and changing jobs all the time instead of having a stable career for their whole lives.

We want them to achieve what we **wanted**
to achieve—and didn't.

We feel we didn't make it, so they're going to have to make it
for us. Of course we'd never admit to anyone that we didn't make
it, and we have a million excuses for why we didn't. Maybe we
didn't study enough in school, for instance, so now our children
have to study extra hard so we can fulfill ourselves through them.

We need to tell ourselves the truth about our own disap-
pointments, failures, and shortcomings—not to make ourselves
wrong but simply so that we won't be unconsciously forcing our
kids to do what we couldn't or wouldn't. If they start to identify
with our failures, then they'll be compelled to offset that apparent imperfection in us somehow. Perhaps they'll never be able
to surpass us in anything. I've heard kids say over and over, "I
can't make that much money. That's more than my Dad made
in his whole lifetime." Others are driven to earn millions of
dollars in order to prove that their dads were failures. In the end,
no one wins.

We want to save **ourselves** *from grief.*

The hardest thing in the world is to experience your child's pain,
whether it's from a breakup with a boyfriend, a bad grade that
means they didn't make the honor roll, not getting on the team,
or something far more difficult—getting arrested for drunk driving, spending some time in jail, or being involved in an incident
in which someone is seriously hurt or killed.

In order to avoid the pain of watching them go through *their*
pain, we will do almost anything. That's usually when we do
the most damage. Our inability to tolerate the sadness of seeing
them sad, or in trouble, causes even more trouble. As usual, we
perpetuate the very things we're trying to avoid.

We want to gain an apparent measure of control.

Watching kids grow up is wonderful, but it's also frightening.

If we can force our own attitudes on them, *make* them accept them, then maybe the kids will start looking more the way they're supposed to look—as though they're turning out "right."

In the end, of course, they will suffer. If they have accepted our attitudes out of reaction or fear without making conscious choices, they won't be able to trust themselves because they won't know how to arrive at a belief. No matter how responsible or self-sufficient they appear to be, they'll be fakes and they'll know it. They'll have to protect and defend their positions forever. They won't know how to make choices about alcohol and other drugs they encounter, or about life itself.

The more common situation is that kids rebel. Here we don't even have the semblance of control that forced acceptance of our attitudes brings, and the child may still grow up knowing very little about making conscious choices. Most of us know at least one fifty-year-old rebel who is still fighting his parents so hard he has no room for his own life.

We've all seen the situation in which the grandchild turns out to be just like the grandparent, the situation in which certain traits seem to "skip a generation." This may be due not only to genetics but also to the decision everybody involved has made that *they are not going to be like their parents*. In fact, they are going to be just the opposite of their parents.

It is quite interesting when your kids start to turn into *your* parents. All the old aggravations come home to roost. That's one of the many reasons it's very important for us to clarify our relationships with our own parents in the process of clarifying our relationships with our children.

ALL ATTITUDES ARE CHOSEN

People will say, "Well, I didn't really choose this or that attitude. That's one I got from my father." That can't be true.

Everybody has attitudes that are the same as their parents', and everybody has attitudes that are different from their parents'. Who chose the different attitudes? If we chose the different ones, we must also have chosen the ones that are the same.

I hear people say, "Oh, I'm a perfectionist because my father made me play the piano eight hours a day and insisted that I do it perfectly." This is like saying, "I was just lying there on the railroad tracks when the train came along. It wasn't my fault!"

Our children choose their own attitudes, too. We aren't the only people with whom they come in contact. They are exposed to many facets of society, and have a great deal more to choose from than we sometimes realize. We need to show them how to identify attitudes so that they can choose them consciously. We then need to let them make those choices for themselves, and not blame them or ourselves or anyone else if they choose something we don't like.

Some people are uncomfortable with being the choosers of their own attitudes. They're afraid that if they can keep rechoosing, then they won't stand for anything at all. People will think they're wishy-washy and uncertain, chameleons without substance. The thing they forget is that they are not their attitudes. Attitudes are attitudes. People are something entirely different.

The process of rechoosing attitudes doesn't mean that we are wishy-washy; it just means that we're operating in present time and doing what's appropriate for now. Say, for example, you have the attitude that drinking and driving don't mix under any circumstances, and that you always stick to your guns. Then one night you're injured at a party fifty miles from anywhere, and the only person who can drive you to the hospital has had a couple of drinks. What do you do? Lie there and bleed to death because drinking and driving don't mix? No, you alter your attitude, rechoose it. You do that because, at least for the moment, the old attitude doesn't serve you.

One of the best ways we can teach our children how to choose among attitudes is to let them observe us as we choose and rechoose our own attitudes. Shifting an attitude does not mean condoning anything. When my daughter repeated to me the amount of alcohol consumed on any given Friday night in her college dorm, I did not change my attitude from condemnation to acceptance. But, given the facts, I did shift it to understanding. Because I did not condemn her or her friends, the communication between us remained open, and my daughter and I could at least discuss the impact on her of what was going on. Rechoosing our attitudes is also a way of demonstrating that we're all simply alive and growing. It's a lot more fun if we let ourselves and one another be exactly where we are in any given moment, and also support one another in moving forward.

We have seen that there are four basic results when we attempt to impose our attitudes on our children:

Communication breaks down as everybody starts reacting rather than responding. Everyone takes positions and we all start playing the survival game of right/wrong.

What we resist is what we get. It's a good bet that our kids will adopt the very attitudes we most want to avoid. The more we resist their having those attitudes, the longer and more strongly they will persist.

Our kids don't "grow up." They have only two options; become carbon copies of us, or become our opposites. They lose their autonomy, their sense of themselves, and their ability to make choices.

They get stuck in either accepting or resisting attitudes that might have been appropriate for our times, but aren't appropriate for their world. They are trying to deal with their world using our attitudes—an inappropriate tool.

WHAT TO DO ABOUT ATTITUDES

We have them, and we're not going to get rid of them. Obviously, it doesn't work well to try to impose our attitudes on our kids. But it's important to remember that trying to "stifle ourselves," as Archie Bunker always advised Edith, won't work, either.

What's the best way to manage those attitudes so that we can live with them without having them run our lives? There are five specific things we can do:

Tell the truth about our attitudes— to ourselves and to our kids.

They already know the truth about us, so it's no news to them. The key, of course, is telling the truth to *ourselves,* bringing our attitudes to the conscious level.

Clare's story illustrates this. Clare's bitterness about her mother's drinking permeated the family atmosphere, but Clare never realized it. She thought her dinnertime lectures on the evils of alcohol, her refusal to have alcohol in the house, and her diatribes against anyone who got tipsy at a family celebration were beneficial to her own children's understanding of the harmful effects of alcohol.

Only when, at a friend's urging, she began attending Alanon (an organization for those affected by another's alcoholism) did she see the truth. Although it took several months for her bitterness to subside, once Clare was aware of her attitude she was able to monitor it. For the first time, her children became willing to discuss alcohol with her rather than sit at the dinner table rolling their eyes around in their heads every time one of her lectures began.

Clare began to be able to say, for example, "I'm dying to tell you not to drink because I've seen what it did to Grandma, but I know you have to go ahead and try it yourself." The hardest part was being willing to see that it might not be a problem for them. And if it was, they could change *as long as she was not standing there saying,* "I told you so!"

Share our attitudes with our kids.
Sharing doesn't mean imposing, nor does it mean confession. It's simply mentioning an interesting thing you noticed about yourself.

When Clare realized the impact her bitter attitude was having on her family she simply said, "I realize that my being upset over Grandma's drinking has been hard on everyone. I want you kids to know that I would hate to have either of you develop alcoholism, but I also see that my negative attitude was enough to drive anyone to drink. I will probably continue to be oversensitive at times, but I do want you to know I can now see what I'm doing, at least part of the time!"

In a sense, you and your kids are embarking together on an adventure in self-discovery.

Don't get sucked into the guilt trip of being a "perfect parent."
Nothing could be more deadly for you or for your child. Trying to be perfect sets up a chain reaction of guilt, victimhood, and righteousness that's devastating. We're going to talk more about this later, but suffice to say that you don't want anything to do with it.

Everybody is somebody's child. That means everybody has a scapegoat. Our kids may be rotten because they had bad parents, but we were bad parents because of our terrible upbringing. It's really *our* parents' fault. It goes right back to Adam and Eve, perhaps beyond.

We're in a position to break that cycle, because we recognize it for what it is. It's a survival mechanism in the right/wrong game, and we can choose whether we want to play or not. The way we break it is to stop blaming our own parents, stop blaming ourselves, and stop blaming our kids. No one is to blame, and everyone is responsible for their own life. It's just that simple, which doesn't mean it's easy.

Examine our attitudes to see if they serve us.

Do they expand our aliveness, our vitality? Or do they restrict and contract our lives? Do they widen our experience, or do they limit it? Do they make us happier and more spontaneous, more able to trust ourselves? Or do they keep us restricted to certain thoughts and behaviors, hemmed into certain boundaries?

An attitude that we have to be perfect parents, for example, will probably be limiting. We edit our thoughts, our feelings, our wants, and our actions so that they will fit into our picture of the perfect parent. An attitude that we are on earth to learn about ourselves and to grow, on the other hand, might turn out to be one that expands our experience of life.

THE BOTTOM LINE IS LOVE

Love is something we haven't talked a great deal about until now, but it underlies everything we've said so far. Why bother to communicate? Why be concerned about what happens to our children? Why want the best for them? Why be committed to them? The answer, of course, is because we love them.

All any of us really wants in life is to be heard, to know that there is someone else out there who can duplicate our experience. When we know that our experience has been duplicated in another person, we have a deeper and fuller experience of ourselves. In a sense, communication is a clearing process.

One way to put it is that love is hearing somebody's experience and wanting them to be all that they want to be. Love is getting ourselves and our attitudes out of the way long enough to duplicate somebody else's experience, and to let them get a glimpse of their potential and their worth.

Let's assume for a minute that the basic motive of everyone who ever dealt with you was love. You don't have to believe it; just hold it as a possibility. If that's the case, all those people who criticized you and made you feel so inadequate were just asking you to be as wonderful as you could possibly be, as wonderful as they knew you could be. Oh sure, they did it all wrong. We all do it wrong, according to somebody, but that's what they really wanted for you.

By the same token, then all your self-criticism really comes out of your love for yourself. You want to be as spectacular as you can be and fulfill as much of yourself as you can. If you recognize that, then instead of castigating yourself for some "fault," you can say, "There's something I'd like to look at. It's no big deal; just an opportunity to see what's behind it."

When I start putting restrictions and demands on you, there's no room for love. Nor is there any room for you to change, because if you changed you might leave me behind or stop fulfilling my needs. Now, that doesn't sound like love to me. If I really love you, I'll let go of you so that you can fulfill yourself.

If I really love you, then I experience something about myself, too. I experience that I am both lovable and "love-able"— able to love. I used to think that lovable involved only being cute or charming or pretty or witty or smart. But love hasn't so much to do with who you are as it has to do with who I am when I'm with you.

Only one thing can stand in the way of the experience of love, and that is fear. It can be fear of other people, fear of not surviving, but mostly it's fear of ourselves. The irony is that we can't really experience anything that doesn't already exist inside ourselves. Whatever is in there can't be all that bad, because we're still around and kicking. We've actually set up a phantom fear, an artificial fear of what might be. It's based on nothing more than the fear of fear, and it keeps us from the thing we want most in life—love.

The nice thing about all this is that we can dissolve fear in a minute, simply by choosing and adopting the attitude that there is nothing within ourselves to fear. There's much to respond to, but nothing to fear. When we know that, we can let go and love.

PART II

ALCOHOL AND OTHER DRUGS

SIX

Alcohol and Other Drugs

THE PURPOSE OF INFORMATION

Since the beginning of time, man has enjoyed altering his consciousness with various substances. Some substances make us excited and stimulated; others make us calm and tranquil. Some create an altered state; others simply relieve anxiety or depression. These substances can help us, or they can hurt us. They hurt us when they keep us from experiencing all of ourselves or our lives.

Having accurate information not only helps us relate to these substances in ways that are beneficial to us, but helps take some of the mystery and "charge" off talking about them. Educating ourselves about alcohol and other drugs is essential to choosing appropriate attitudes and to helping our children to choose them. That is the purpose of this chapter.

HISTORY OF ALCOHOL
IN THE NEW WORLD

There has never been a shortage of alcohol in the New World. Beer came over on the Mayflower in 1620. The Spanish missionaries brought grapevines to America and, before we were even a nation, there was wine making in California. The Dutch opened the first distillery on Staten Island in 1640. Brewing was nearly as important as milling and baking in the Massachusetts Bay Colony. We think of the Puritans as never touching alcohol, but that was not the case. In 1790, a federal law was passed rationing to each soldier a fourth pint of brandy, rum, or whiskey per day.

Beer, wine, and liquor were all used by the colonists, but it was rum from Jamaica that became the standard drink. To get rum, New Englanders engaged in the slave trade that supplied the molasses needed to produce it. The Scotch and Irish settlers in Kentucky, West Virginia, and Maryland made whiskey (the backwoods substitute for rum), and it soon became even more popular than rum. Sour-mash bourbon became America's favorite drink.

An early Connecticut law forbade drinking for more than a half hour at a time, but attitudes toward alcohol were fairly low-key in our country's early years. Drinking didn't become a real issue in American society until the opening of the West. According to Kinney and Leaton, in *Loosening the Grip, A Handbook of Alcohol Information:*

> Drinking in the colonies was largely a family affair and remained so until the beginning of the nineteenth century. With increasing immigration, industrialization, and greater social freedom, drinking became less a family affair. The abuse of alcohol became more open and more destructive. The opening of the West brought the saloon into prominence. The old and stable social and family patterns began to change. The frontier hero took to gulping his drinks with his foot on the barrail. Attitudes began to intensify regarding the use of alcohol, the stigma of alcoholism, the wet-dry controversy. Ways of looking at alcohol began to polarize in America. The legal

and moral approaches reached their apex in the United States with the growth of the temperance movement and the Prohibition amendment in 1919.

Temperance began as part of the rising social conscience in the nineteenth century, a humanitarian movement that included women's rights, abolition of slavery, and child labor laws. In 1874 Frances Willard founded the Women's Christian Temperance Union. It sponsored mass meetings and programs that taught fear and hatred of alcohol. The Anti-Saloon League followed, and was a powerful force behind any Prohibitionist candidate.

In 1919 Congress passed the Eighteenth Amendment (Prohibition), which made it illegal to manufacture or sell alcoholic beverages. Prohibition was in effect from 1920 to 1933. It was during this time that many of the myths, and the "forbidden" mystique surrounding alcohol got started.

DRUGS IN THE UNITED STATES

Narcotics

Opium was available legally, conveniently, and cheaply throughout the Civil War, and heroin was marketed openly toward the end of the nineteenth century. You could buy narcotics over-the-counter at drug stores, groceries, and general stores, or you could get a prescription from your doctor.

A survey of Iowa stores during the years 1883 to 1885 revealed that opium was on sale at 3,000 stores. You could get opiates through mail order, and many of the patent medicines of the day (including "Mrs. Winslow's Soothing Syrup" and "Ayers Cherry Pectoral") contained opium or morphine. They purported to cure anything from teething pain to "women's troubles," and I just bet they did! During the nineteenth century, most opium was imported legally, or processed legally in America. It wasn't until 1942 that

Congress banned the cultivation of opium poppies. San Francisco prohibited smoking opium in "dens" in 1875, but the ban had more to do with racism than it did with health. Tens of thousands of Chinese had come to the area in the 1850s and 1860s to build the great western railroads. They drifted to the cities, and soon white men and women were smoking opium side by side with the Chinese.

Despite strong disapproval of this racial mixing from all quarters, the law was ineffective and people kept right on doing it. Finally, in 1887, Congress raised tariffs and prohibited the importation by Chinese of the kind of opium used to produce smoking opium. Three years later, a law was passed that limited the manufacture of smoking opium to American citizens. Again, it was racism rather than any interest in limiting people's opium consumption. It was fine if Caucasian Americans manufactured and imported it; they just didn't want the Chinese doing it.

In 1914 the Harrison Act was passed to set guidelines for the orderly marketing of opium, morphine, heroin, and other narcotics, and was later converted into a law prohibiting the supplying of narcotics to addicts. With these substances made illegal, the addict subculture and criminal underground began to flourish.

Cocaine

When the Spanish conquistadors arrived in the early sixteenth century, they found the Incas chewing the leaves of a mountain shrub called *erythroxylon* coca, which produced euphoria and a highly energized state. A local nobleman used the coca leaves to control the natives, distributing them to the Indians so that they would work harder and longer on less food.

People in Europe and America never took to chewing the leaves, but they developed several drinks from the coca plant. One of these was "Mariani's wine," which became very popular in Europe. In 1885 a former patent medicine salesman from Atlanta, Georgia, named John Styth Pemberton, began market-

ing a product similar to Mariani's wine called "French Wine Coca–
Ideal Nerve and Tonic Stimulant." The next year he added another coca product to his line: Coca-Cola. In the United States,
cocaine was widely used not only in Coca-Cola but in tonics and
other patent medicines, particularly those claiming to cure ca-
tarrh. The Pure Food and Drug Act passed in 1906 forced Pemberton to switch from ordinary coca leaves to decocainized coca
leaves, so there is no cocaine in Coke today.

Amphetamines

Amphetamines were first synthesized in 1887, but weren't marketed until 1932. They were used primarily to combat narcolepsy, a disease whose victims fall asleep many times a day
without any notice, right in the middle of whatever they are doing.

During World War II, American, British, German, and Jap-
anese military units issued amphetamines to their men to counteract fatigue, elevate mood, and heighten endurance. After the war,
physicians routinely prescribed amphetamines for depression, and
a modest black market grew up alongside the expanding legal
market for prescribed amphetamines. Early black market users
included truck drivers and students, who took them while cram-
ming for exams. The use of amphetamines by athletes and busi-
nessmen (and their secretaries) was reported as early as 1940.

In 1965, new amendments to the federal food and drug laws
were designed to curb the black market in amphetamines. This
made it harder for the black market to acquire legally manufactured amphetamines, but at the same time provided a great impetus to their illegal manufacture in kitchens and garages across
the country.

Speed

During the Korean War, servicemen learned to mix amphetamines with heroin and to inject the combination into their veins.
They brought the practice home with them, and speed—the in-
travenous injection of large doses of amphetamines—has be-

come perhaps the most potentially hazardous form of drug use yet devised.

Methamphetamine (Methedrine) injections were used in the late 1950s as treatment for heroin addiction. Doctors would sell the drug and the needles to heroin addicts, who would then sell the Methedrine for a profit on the street to support their heroin habit.

In the early 1960s, it was commonplace for pharmacies around San Francisco to sell injectable amphetamines without a prescription, or with a crudely forged prescription. The practice continued until a scandal broke in 1962. The offshoot of all the publicity was to create a great interest in, and a large body of knowledge about, mainlining amphetamines. The anti-drug propaganda only served to popularize speed. Everyone was railing against speed, marijuana, and LSD. Since the kids were convinced marijuana was not only harmless but great, they figured the "establishment" was putting them on about speed, too.

Meanwhile, as soon as the scandals broke, many manufacturers took their amphetamines off the retail market and sold them to hospitals. The black market got vast quantities of nonsterile amphetamines for a fraction of their actual cost, since the manufacturers had lost the pharmacy market. Their only competition now were the "speed labs" popping up all over the San Francisco Bay Area.

Only when Allen Ginsberg, Timothy Leary, the Beatles, and the Mothers of Invention spoke out against speed did people start to listen.

LSD

LSD (lysergic acid diethylamide, or LSD-25) was discovered by Dr. Albert Hofman, a chemist working in Switzerland, in 1938. It was studied and ingested by many psychiatrists, physcians, and psychologists, but for some time its uses remained undefined. The U.S. Army experimented with it for possible use in brainwashing and getting prisoners to talk more freely, and for disabling enemy forces. Some psychiatrists gave it to their staffs so that they could understand their patients better, because it was supposed that LSD induced a psychotic state. Others gave it to their patients as an aid to psychotherapy, because it was thought to reduce the patient's resistance. LSD became available for personal use in the 1950s, and this use became more widespread during the 1960s.

PCP

PCP was first studied in 1957 as a potential anesthetic, but was considered too dangerous and disorienting for human use. It was used chiefly as an anesthetic for large animals until it appeared on the streets during the 1967 "summer of love" in San Francisco. Its unpredictable and unpleasant side effects gave it a bad reputation, and it was not used knowingly for some years. By 1974, however, it had resurfaced as a popular drug and its use at present is said to have reached epidemic proportions.

THE LAST TWENTY YEARS

The 1960s were the "drug years." Drugs were newly popular with middle-class kids. Drugs were "in," anti-establishment, and produced states of consciousness never experienced by their parents or by the people who were making the war in Vietnam. Haight-Ashbury in San Francisco became a mecca for the drug culture.

Parents had such a strong reaction to their children's use of marijuana, LSD, and heroin that these substances became all the more attractive. Alcohol was seldom thought of or referred to as a drug, and parents longed for the good old days when high-school students would just go out and get drunk, instead of hanging out with and possibly becoming "drug-crazed hippie freaks." If their children "just drank," parents counted themselves lucky and figured they must have done something right. Further polarization took place as parents sat around their suburban living rooms drinking martinis and taking Valium—while chastizing their kids for smoking pot.

The 1970s brought a return to alcohol, for a combination of reasons. Partly it was just the pendulum swinging back. Bucking the establishment became less important, a less significant part of growing up. The economy was starting to slump, and alcohol was cheaper than many drugs. Parents leaned back and heaved a sigh of relief.

What no one noticed at first was that children were starting to drink at younger and younger ages, even in grammar school. This was so alien to parents' own experience that they had trouble accepting that it was true. Alcoholism among children in their early teens was becoming not a rarity or an aberration, but a fairly common phenomenon.

With the 1980s, there has come a partial return to other drugs. Alcohol remains the drug of choice, however, especially when mixed with other drugs. Marijuana and cocaine are another of the most popular "mixes." The combination of alcohol and other drugs presents new problems because of the synergistic effect that can take place when they are mixed.

Synergism is the whole becoming greater than the sum of its parts. When alcohol is mixed with barbiturates, for instance, the result will produce a reaction stronger than the effect of the barbiturate and the effect of the alcohol combined. It's a case of one and one equaling not two, but four or six!

This is one of the many reasons it's essential for our children to be informed about alcohol and other drugs, and the various ways they may find them put together. They have to know what they're being offered before they can make responsible choices about it.

ALCOHOL: WHAT IS IT?

Alcohol is a drug. It is a depressant that works on the central nervous system (brain and spinal cord). We sometimes think of alcohol as a stimulant, because we've seen people get loud and raucous when they drink. Actually, what's happening is that the part of their brain that controls judgment and inhibitions is being depressed.

Alcohol is also an irritant to both the gastrointestinal system and the central nervous system. It is an anesthetic (kills pain and puts you "under"), an analgesic (kills pain), and an antiseptic (kills germs and fights infection).

Alcohol has specific, measurable effects on the mind and body in both the short and long term. Let's follow a drop (or several drops) of alcohol through the system of someone we'll call Jack, and see step by step what happens inside his body and mind when he goes to a party and has a few drinks:

It's Friday night, and Jack has had a tough week. He tried two cases in court and he's ready to relax. So is his wife, Betty, who works part-time at the local hospital and manages the house and their two children. They're both ready to let their hair down a bit, so they're delighted to be going to a party.

The first thing that happens when they arrive is that they accept drinks from their genial host, Horace. Jack has a Scotch and water, and Betty has a glass of wine.

Jack takes his first sip of Scotch and smiles. He may not know it, but lots of things are already starting to happen inside his body. As soon as the alcohol touches Jack's lips, small amounts of it are absorbed into the bloodstream through tiny capillaries in the mouth, but most of it proceeds on to his stomach. There, it acts as an irritant, and also increases the flow of hydrochloric acid, a digestive juice secreted by the stomach lining.

In most people, this is what produces that warm glow. It isn't much fun for Jack, though. He's starting to get ulcers, and the last thing they need is to be irritated. He gets over that quickly, however, because of alcohol's anesthetic property. As the alcohol leaves Jack's stomach, 20 percent of it has already been absorbed into his bloodstream.

Jack had a big dinner, so the alcohol is absorbed more slowly than it would be if he hadn't eaten all that hamburger and broccoli and potatoes. Alcohol is absorbed more quickly on an empty stomach; when the drink has a high concentration of alcohol per ounce (this is why straight whiskey has more of a "kick" than wine or beer); and when carbon dioxide is present, as it is in champagne, sparkling wines, and drinks mixed with soda.

If Jack tossed down several drinks, one after another, something else might happen at this point in the alcohol's journey through the body. The pylorus valve, which controls the movement of substances from the stomach to the small intestine, might close. The pylorus valve is sensitive to alcohol, and closes when the concentration of alcohol is very high in order to protect the rest of the system from that much toxic substance. The alcohol remains trapped in the stomach and the result is that the stomach usually gets irritated enough that the person vomits. In essence, the pylorus valve has said, "Hey, enough! Stop the music! This body can't take any more poison now!" But Jack doesn't drink that much that quickly. The alcohol continues on into his small intestine, where the remaining 70 percent is absorbed into his bloodstream.

Alcohol doesn't have to be digested, like other foods. It goes immediately into the bloodstream through the walls of the intestines. Within thirty seconds, it hits the brain. This is what produces the feeling of being "high." The alcohol is already starting to depress some of the areas of the brain, especially in the frontal lobe. The things we forget most quickly and easily when we drink are the things we've learned most recently. One of the many reasons drinking and driving is even more deadly for teens than it is for adults is that they have learned to drive more recently than we have. (They have also practiced less.)

At any rate, the alcohol is now traveling throughout Jack's system via his blood and the water in his cells. It permeates all his cells, and goes wherever there is fluid in the body, which is just about everywhere. The brain is about 85 percent fluid, so it gets hit pretty hard.

Jack is feeling great, though. He says, "I feel much more like I do now than I did when I came in!" People's heads whirl around and they say, "What?!" Jack just smiles. Horace offers him another drink, and he accepts. His blood pressure is getting higher now, his heart rate increasing, and his blood alcohol level is starting to rise.

BLOOD ALCOHOL LEVELS

Blood alcohol levels (BALs) measure the amount of alcohol in the system. Alcohol is soluble in water and is distributed evenly thoughout the body tissues wherever there is fluid. The concentration of fluid is highest in the brain, liver, and muscle.

A BAL of .10 percent means that .10 percent is the concentration of alcohol to water in the tissues. In most states, a person with a BAL of .10 percent is considered legally intoxicated. It indicates that the person weighing about 175 pounds has probably had five drinks in the first hour—or six drinks in two hours.

Obviously, it will take more drinks to get a 250-pound person to a BAL of .10 percent than it will to get a 100-pound person to .10 percent. There is more fluid in the 250-pound person, more volume to absorb the same amound of alcohol.

It also takes more alcohol to get a man to .10 percent than a woman, possibly because women have a higher percentage of fat to muscle than men do, and alcohol is not fat-soluble. This means that a lower percentage of her total volume is able to absorb the alcohol, so her concentration of alcohol would be higher with the same amount. Women also absorb alcohol more quickly just before their menstrual period and when they are taking birth control pills. The impact on children of a .10 percent BAL is extremely serious. Young bodies are still in formation and the damage to the brain and other organs, from excessive alcohol, is far greater than to those of an adult. The rule for giving young children alcohol, even a taste of your beer, is—don't! All too often I have seen parents chortling over the antics of a slightly tipsy toddler who is wandering around the patio polishing off the dregs of beer cans. To put it bluntly, this is not only not funny, it is extremely dangerous.

What do the various BALs mean? How many drinks does it take to get drunk? This varies from person to person according to metabolism, size, and sex, but the following chart gives you a general idea. This chart is not applicable to those afflicted with alcoholism. I'll explain why later.

MALE - 175 POUNDS

Drinks per Hour	BAL	Condition
1	.02%	relaxed, loose
2.5	.05%	impaired judgment, inhibitions slightly suspended, some loss of coordination
5	.10%	little or no judgment, poor coordination, legally drunk, erratic emotions, impaired vision
10	.20%	emotions out of control, lack of coordination, memory affected
1 pint	.40%	stuporous, no judgment or coordination
1.25 pints	.65%	coma, death

"Drink" is defined as ½ ounce of alcohol, which translates into 4½ ounces of wine, 12 ounces of beer, or 1¼ ounces of whiskey. This is how the concentration of alcohol in these drinks might look:

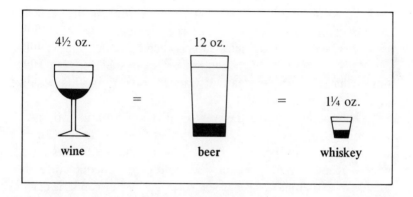

(Of course the alcohol isn't all down at the bottom, as it appears to be in the picture. The kids in my classes always joke about that. They say they'll just drink the top half so they won't get any alcohol!) You also have to be careful about what a "drink" is. I don't think I owned a shot glass. I'd just turn the bottle upside down over the glass until it looked sort of full or felt like enough. You'd probably get three or four times what a "drink" is on that chart, and I'm not the only person who pours drinks that way!

Another thing to remember is that, as the evening wears on, people often think the bartender or their host is lightening up the drinks, not putting as much alcohol in them. They forget that their taste buds and sense of smell have been dulled by all the alcohol they've drunk, and that it takes much more alcohol to produce the same taste and smell they experienced with their first drink of the evening. For this reason, there is actually a tendency to pour *heavier* drinks as time goes by.

REMOVAL

Jack has now had about three drinks. His judgment isn't quite what it normally is, and he starts cozying up to his best friend's wife. He's feeling a little euphoric, as if the world isn't really such a bad place after all. He isn't exactly slurring his speech, but his emotions are closer to the surface and his coordination isn't what it was forty minutes earlier when he came in the door.

Betty suggests he have a cup of coffee to sober up, but Jack thinks that's a terrible idea and wanders off to give his boss a piece of his mind.

There is a myth that the way to sober up a drunk is by giving him coffee. Nothing could be further from the truth. Coffee has no effect on a person's BAL, which is the key to his level of intoxication. What you get when you give someone coffee is a wide-awake drunk. Nor can you sober up by "sweating it out." Only 10 percent of the alcohol is processed out of the body through the breath, sweat, and urine combined—no matter how much you sweat.

The liver is the key element in eliminating alcohol from the system. It's the primary detoxifier, and the liver needs time to work—about one hour per drink. It handles the 90 percent not processed through the breath, sweat, and urine. The liver changes alcohol into acetaldehyde, then acetic acid, and finally into carbon dioxide and water.

Large amounts of alcohol in the system don't make the liver work any faster. The liver's job is to take toxic substances in the system and detoxify them, and it pursues that job very steadily and methodically. It works at the same rate no matter what is in the body, and it will always take the most toxic substance first. In the liver's judgment, you can't get more toxic than alcohol. This means that any other substances that have to be processed in the liver—fats, for example—have to "wait in line" if the liver is busy processing lots of alcohol.

This is how people who drink a lot develop "fatty livers."

While the liver is busy with all that alcohol, the fat from any butter or hamburgers they might have eaten has to wait, and starts piling up in the liver. The accumulated fat eventually causes scar tissue, which is essentially what cirrhosis is.

WITHDRAWAL

But enough about livers for now. Back to Jack. He's tossed down five drinks in an hour, which means his BAL is about .10 percent, so he decides to start taking it easy. Interestingly, ever since he took the first drink and his alcohol level started going up, the alcohol was also being metabolized out of his body. Now that he's slowed down, the BAL is starting to drop and the withdrawal process starts to take place.

A BAL of .06 percent on the way down is a lot different, and a lot less fun, than a BAL of .06 percent on the way up. I don't mean that Jack is stretched out on a cot with the delirium tremens. You don't have to have gone that far to appreciate what happens when you've been drinking quite a bit and then you stop. The central nervous system has been depressed, but now it gets irritated. Jack's brain and nerves get excited, irritable, cranky. He starts to feel edgy.

This can happen even if you've literally passed out. You feel as though your mind is going a mile a minute. If you've simply "fallen asleep," you can get insomnia, or you might have wild dreams. So now poor Jack's nervous system is depressed and irritated at the same time, which is a very unpleasant state. What would relieve it? Jack thinks about this for a minute, and comes up with the answer, "Another drink!" Unfortunately, he's right.

DRUNK VERSUS
INTOXICATED

About an hour and a half after he got to the party, Jack has his sixth drink. Many of his faculties are affected now—his judgment; his coordination; his senses of speech, vision, and touch; his emotions; even his autonomic nervous system, which controls such involuntary life functions as heart and respiration.

Jack holds his liquor well, though. He doesn't look sloppy. He doesn't look like someone you'd expect to see slumped on a park bench clutching a bottle of Tokay wine. His BAL is about .09 percent, but he doesn't look bad.

Betty, meanwhile, has been off with some friends catching up on the gossip and has had about three glasses of wine. Since she's a lot smaller than Jack and is a woman, that just might bring her BAL up to about .10 percent too. In terms of the amount of alcohol they've consumed, relative to their body sizes and sex, they have kept about even with one another.

When Jack looks up and sees Betty walking toward him, she has a lampshade on her head. Betty is really ripped, almost falling-down drunk, and feels numb all over.

Now, whom would you choose to drive you home, Jack or Betty? Most of us would choose Jack, but the truth is that he is just as intoxicated as Betty. He has just as much toxic material, relative to his size, in his system as she does. He just isn't showing it as much. She is drunk, but they're both intoxicated. Jack isn't spilling drinks, and he might even be able to walk a straight line. Nonetheless, things are happening inside his body over which he has no control.

Alcohol affects vision, for example. One thing that happens is we lose our ability to track small objects, like animals and children. If something darts out into the road, we won't always see it.

Alcohol also affects the cones of the eyes and the constriction and dilation of the pupils. One evening at a party a friend of mine in the highway patrol gave me a sobriety test. I had had close to a bottle of champagne but I had no trouble passing most of the obvious tests. I could walk a straight line, stand on one foot and touch my nose and say the alphabet. However, when he shone a flashlight in my eyes, my pupils didn't constrict. The reflexes were slowed down considerably because of all the booze in my system. My pupils just sat there, not knowing what to do, but when he took the light away a few seconds later, they decided to close. Delayed reaction. The effect of the alcohol was that my pupils were wide open when they should have been shut, and shut when they should have been open, which blinded me and certainly would have had a serious effect on my driving.

Alcohol also affects your sense of touch. It's an anesthetic. It makes you numb. That's why alcoholics can wake up in the morning with bruises all over their bodies and not even know where the bruises came from. Alcohol also causes disintegration of the reticular activating system, which affects our balance and coordination.

So even if someone is standing at the bar looking smooth and suave, all these things are going on inside him. He can be just as intoxicated as the person with the lampshade on her head, but he might not be acting drunk. Drunkeness is a behavior; intoxication is a physical state of toxicity.

UNPLEASANT EFFECTS

Jack and Betty finally get home (in a cab, thanks to Horace), and the next day they feel just terrible. They're not aware of all the things that are happening inside their bodies. All they know is that they've been run over by a Mack truck. They swear they'll never drink again, and spend the day in bed recuperating.

I've designed some technical terminology for some of the effects Jack and Betty are experiencing.

Thirsty but bloated.

Have you ever felt as though your body were bloated, but still you couldn't get enough water to drink? That is due to the process of osmosis that occurs when there is alcohol in your system. The water inside your cells moves *outside* the cells. The result is that there's a lot of water in your body, which makes you feel bloated, but the cells themselves are crying for water. They're sending your brain the message that they're dying of thirst—and they are.

Squished brain.

This term may not be used in medical literature, but it describes what happens when alcohol makes the blood vessels in the brain dilate. This causes the brain to actually expand and press up against the skull. Talk about headaches! Squished brain is a temporary condition, because the blood vessels eventually go back to their normal size. The brain cells we smash in the process generally regenerate. We have billions and billions of brain cells, so losing a few won't destroy us. However, we don't know exactly which particular parts of the brain are going to get squished. It might be something we don't want right away, but it might be a part containing important information. It's a little like playing Russian roulette. You never really know which cells will be damaged or what effect that damage will produce.

Pickled brain.

Another of my technical terms. Every single time we take a drink, even one small glass of white wine, some of our brain cells die. Again, that's not serious because we have so many of them and don't use most of them anyway. It's not something to take a lot of chances with, however. When you have those brain cells being exposed over and over again to saturation with alcohol, even the ones that live are apt to be a little the worse for wear because they're being pickled repeatedly.

Sticky blood.

After exposure to alcohol, your blood cells tend to stick together. It is very difficult for oxygen to be carried by them. The brain depends on blood cells for its oxygen, so this situation is a lot more serious than squished brain. Sometimes squished brain cells can regenerate, but cells that don't receive oxygen can't. In the long term, we're talking about serious brain damage.

Blackout
A blackout has occurred if you wake up the next morning and can't remember what happened the night before. It is even more serious when the blackout has a blackout: You don't remember that you don't remember. Someone calls up and tells you all the things you did, and you weren't even aware that you had lost part of the evening.

Korsakoff's syndrome.
This is irreversible brain damage and is called, less technically, "wet brain." At this stage, a person has virtually become a vegetable. For most people, it doesn't come to this. They usually die before they get to this point.

Heart
Some physicians say that a little alcohol is good for the heart, but others disagree. They say that speeding up the heart rate, raising blood pressure, and constricting the blood vessels of the heart can overload the organ. Some researchers say that two ounces of alcohol impedes the flow of blood to your heart. The long-term effects on the heart are enlargement, decreased pumping ability, arrythmia, and cellular death.

Liver
We've already talked a little about what happens to the liver when it's forced to detoxify alcohol while everything else waits in line and backs up. The liver always processes the most toxic substance first, and it considers alcohol even more toxic than barbiturates. If you've combined alcohol and barbiturates, there-

fore, you may be in for more reaction than you bargained for because the barbiturates will have to wait in line to be detoxified and will be in your system far longer than you may have planned.

The fatty liver that occurs when foods such as meat and butter have to wait their turn, is reversible. Serious trouble begins when the buildup of fatty tissue results in the development of scar tissue.

The liver's insistence on metabolizing alcohol first can also throw the body into a hypoglycemic state. Sugar is the only source of energy the brain cells can use. While the liver is removing alcohol from the system, it can't manufacture and release glucose (sugar) into the bloodstream. This is all right if you have just eaten, but between meals it can deprive the brain of its proper nourishment. The symptoms are hunger, weakness, perspiration, headache, nervousness, and tremors. If allowed to continue, this condition can result in coma.

Nerves
The effect here is not merely getting a little more nervous, but the degeneration of the sheaths of the nerves. People have become quadriplegics from this process. Some people's bodies have become so sensitive that they can't put sheets over themselves without causing pain. This syndrome is called polyneuritis, which causes a prickly feeling and numbness, as well as pain.

Because alcohol acts as a depressant and an irritant on the central nervous system, it interferes with or lowers the activity of the brain. The first parts affected are the frontal lobe and the "newer" parts of the brain—those affecting judgment and inhibition.

As I mentioned before, there is also memory loss, starting in those areas where most recent learning occurred. In other words, what you learned yesterday will be lost before what you learned ten years ago.

Choking

If you ever see someone lying on his back or stomach after he's passed out from drinking, turn him over on his side. A startling number of deaths are caused by people choking and drowning on their own regurgitation. This is more likely to happen if they've combined the alcohol with a drug like Quaalude, Valium, or cocaine. People are also more likely to choke on food when they're drinking. Their natural coughing reflex is depressed due to the alcohol. After you've turned the person over on his side, get help, of course.

Delirium tremens. (DTs)

Prior to modern methods of detoxification, delirium tremens were a cause of death in 20 to 25 percent of those who experienced them. DTs are caused by the sudden withdrawal of alcohol from an addicted body. They are a cataclysmic body response characterized by convulsions, sweating, and hallucinations. The fatal nature of alcohol withdrawal is second only to withdrawal from barbiturates.

SHORT-TERM AND LONG-TERM EFFECTS OF ALCOHOL

To summarize what we've said so far, alcohol is a drug that acts as a depressant and as an irritant on the central nervous system. It is an anesthetic, an analgesic, and an antiseptic. The short-term effects of drinking alcohol are loss of control over:

Judgment, reason, inhibitions
Emotions
Coordination and reflexes
Senses
(vision, hearing, speech, touch, taste, and smell)

Autonomic nervous system
(involuntary responses like heartbeat, breathing, etc.)
Vital systems
(heart and respiratory), causing death

In the long term, drinking alcohol has many implications: emotional, physical, mental, spiritual, social, and legal. Emotionally, it puts the drinker on a roller coaster. It's up and down, up and down, with the physical effects sometimes producing guilt, producing the desire to drink more, and so forth.

Physically, the main areas where deterioration takes place are the liver, heart, cardiovascular system, pancreas, and brain. Mentally, consumption of large amounts of alcohol over long periods of time affects memory, learning capacity, self-esteem, and ability to function independently.

The areas in which alcohol meets the law are primarily DWI (driving while intoxicated), homicide, suicide, incest, rape and family fights. It is estimated that alcohol played a role in about half of the 60,000 highway deaths each year. Chronic drinkers who had more than one offense were responsible for two-thirds of these fatalities. Forty percent of the pedestrians killed had been drinking, and 32 percent of the pedestrians and 53 percent of the drivers had alcohol levels of over .10 percent.*

Over one-half of all homicides are alcohol related. Two-thirds of all assaults and felonies are committed by people who have been drinking. Almost half of the 5.5 million arrests made each year in the United States are related to the misuse of alcohol. Alcohol is a contributing factor in over half of all child abuse cases. Statistics involving sexual assault are just now being studied, but in one southwestern state, it was reported that half of all the convicted rapists had been drinking prior to the rape, and 35 percent were considered to be alcoholic. Another study

*Loosening the Grip, A Handbook of Alcohol Information

of men involved in child molesting found half were drunk and one-third were alcoholic.*

Police report that alcohol is a universal factor in the family fights they handle. Drunkenness accounts for about a million and a half arrests each year and costs the taxpayers about $100 million, and violent crime costs over $3 billion.

THE ADVANTAGES OF ALCOHOL

Despite all this, there are members of the medical profession who think that moderate amounts of alcohol can be helpful. Their research shows that people who abstain from alcohol do not live longer than people who drink moderately. By moderately, they mean a maximum of one ounce of pure alcohol a day (two "drinks," by our previous definition). Once people start to drink beyond that, their mortality rate increases very quickly.

Other advantages are that alcohol is a social lubricant, a relaxer, and a tranquilizer. Some people make the argument that those sorts of lubricants shouldn't be necessary, but others would argue that if they bring people closer together, then they work.

THE DISADVANTAGES OF
ALCOHOL FOR YOUNG PEOPLE

One of the major disadvantages of alcohol for young people is the combination of drinking and driving. The three things you need to be able to do well in order to drive safely are: 1) see, 2) decide, and 3) act. Alcohol impairs all three of these functions. When your vision, judgment, and coordination are affected, you make faulty judgments based on something you're seeing inaccurately, and then react to all of this with impaired reflexes.

*Loosening the Grip, A Handbook of Alcohol Information

Remember that at a BAL of .10 percent, you are intoxicated whether or not you're staggering around. Add to that the fact that young people usually don't have as much experience with drinking or with driving as those of us who have been doing both for a longer time, and the potential for the most recently acquired knowledge to go first when drinking, and you have a very dangerous situation.

Besides the damage that alcohol can do in the emotional, physical, mental, spiritual, and legal spheres, alcohol is obviously the thing that triggers alcoholism That doesn't mean that if you drink, you're headed for alcoholism; but you can't become an alcoholic without drinking.

ALCOHOL AND OTHER DRUGS

For centuries, people have been looking for ways to alter the feelings of pain, anxiety, nervousness, depression, and other emotions that they consider unpleasant. They have been successful. There are now so many substances to change the way you feel that it's difficult to name them all.

A lot of people get upset at the very mention of drugs, and that may well be the single largest barrier to communicating with our kids about them. It's difficult to respond to something that scares you. I've found that the best way to lose fear about something is to learn about it.

When people think of drugs, they often think of addiction. That's a mysterious area to most of us. We have a lot of misconceptions about it. *Licit and Illicit Drugs* defines an addicting drug as "one that most users continue to take even though they want to stop, decide to stop, try to stop, and actually succeed in stopping for days, week, months, or even years." My definition is that any substance which makes one feel "more normal," which one continues to take regardless of negative consequences, and which causes physical or psychological pain upon withdrawal, is an addictive substance for that person.

More and more people, adults as well as children, are mixing the drugs they take with alcohol. The problem with combining alcohol with other drugs is that not only are you dealing with two substances instead of one, but the ways in which the two drugs combine can be volatile and unpredictable. One way to avoid such trouble is to be informed about the various drugs available today and what happens when they are combined with each other and with alcohol.

Most drugs have several effects—sometimes contradictory effects which make classifying them difficult. Cocaine, for example, is a CNS (central nervous system) stimulant and depressant. PCP (phencyclidine), a sedative, stimulant, and hallucinogen; alcohol, a stimulant, irritant, and depressant. However, for the sake of simplifying things they will be classed in their predominant mode.

Marijuana

Marijuana is the dried leaves and flowers of the cannabis plant. Of all the drugs we will discuss, the least is known about marijuana, although it has been used for thousands of years. It does not fit exactly into the usual categories of drugs, although some regard it as a mild hallucinogen. Marijuana can be smoked or ingested. It enters the bloodstream and acts on the brain and nervous system. Its effects are felt usually within fifteen minutes and last two to four hours.

Marijuana affects mood, judgment, and thinking. It can produce euphoria, relaxation, depression, gregariousness, sleepiness, or excitement, depending on the individual and the dosage. Time and space are distorted, often judgment is impaired, and the abilities to concentrate and think clearly are diminished. Some people have reduced coordination and reflexes. A few people report hallucinations. Chronic users often experience lack of motivation, impairment of memory, and decreased learning capacity.

The reproductive system may also be affected. Some studies have revealed reduced hormones in both sexes, increase in the number of abnormally-shaped sperm, blockage of ovulation, and disruption of menstrual cycles.

The effects of marijuana on the lungs seems to be slightly more damaging than the effects of tar and nicotine.

It is not a good idea to drive or to do anything requiring concentration or coordination after smoking marijuana. Long-term effects seem to be primarily psychological, ranging from depression to dependency.

When combined with alcohol, as it quite often is, marijuana has an additive effect. That is, the user would experience the effects of alcohol and the effects of marijuana at the same time. The primary mind-altering ingredient in marijuana is THC (delta-9-tetrahydrocannabinol). A major danger is that THC in concentrated chemical form turns off the brain's "vomit center." This could result in people not being aware that they are drinking more alcohol than their bodies can handle.

Cocaine
Cocaine (coke, snow, lady, or gold dust) is extracted from the leaves of the South American coca plant. It stimulates the central nervous system and produces a sense of euphoria and well-being. It is commonly ingested by inhaling it in powder form so that it is absorbed by the nasal membranes.

Cocaine has a subtle and deceptive effect when mixed with alcohol. Most people think of cocaine as an upper, because it gives them such a rush. There is an intial rush with cocaine, and even difficulty in falling asleep after the drug has been taken, but then the reverse happens. It depresses the respiratory system. This depression of the respiratory system can be so severe that breathing stops. People don't realize they're taking that much cocaine, because its depressive effects aren't at all obvious in the beginning. When they're taking it, it feels like (and is) a stimulant.

When you combine this depressive quality with alcohol, which is also a depressant, you have the potential for a "double depressant," which gives no warning. The "coming down" depressant effect of the cocaine combines with the depressant effect of the alcohol, and people can and do die of respiratory failure. They simply stop breathing. Also, death can occur as the result of encephalitis from untreated nasal infection caused by destruction of the septum.

One of the chief problems with cocaine is that people have been told it is nonaddictive. *Cocaine is addictive,* as thousands and thousands of people will attest. In *Licit and Illicit Drugs,* Edward Brecher tells how cocaine addiction works:

> Cocaine addiction differs from opiate addiction and from alcohol and barbiturate addiction in at least two respects. A cocaine user, even after prolonged use of large doses, does not, if deprived of his drug, suffer from a dramatic withdrawal crisis like alcoholic delirium tremens or like the opiate withdrawal syndrome. The physiological effects of cocaine withdrawal are minor. This has led many authorities, mistakenly, to classify cocaine as a nonaddicting drug. However, cocaine withdrawal is characterized by a profound psychological manifestation—depression—for which cocaine itself appears to the user to be the only remedy. Cocaine addiction in this respect resembles tobacco addiction more closely than it resembles opiate or alcohol addiction. The compulsion to resume cocaine is very strong.

As we will discuss later, any psychological dependence is in fact physical.

Heroin

Heroin, known in street terms as horse, smack, or junk, is classified as a narcotic and acts on the central nervous system as well as the internal organs. It comes from the opium poppy and is a white, off-white, or brown crystalline powder. It can be sniffed, smoked, or injected into a vein or muscle.

The immediate effects are feeling a flush, especially in the abdomen, and constriction of the pupils. Soon the user feels drowsy, euphoric, and blissful. There are dream-like states in which he drifts in and out of various realities. Onlookers would describe him as looking dazed.

Common side effects are constipation, anxiety, fear, restlessness, nausea, shortness of breath, vomiting, and dizziness. An overdose can lead to coma and death by respiratory failure.

Heroin addicts develop a cross-tolerance to other drugs. In other words, their tolerance for heroin translates into a tolerance (and possible addiction) to other drugs.

There is a close relationship between alcoholism and heroin addiction. Studies of ex-heroin addicts show that nearly half become alcoholics, and that many nondrinking or "recovered" alcoholics become heroin addicts.

LSD

LSD (lysergic acid diethylamide) is a hallucinogen. It is usually taken orally in drops, sugar cubes, tablets, squares of gelatin ("window pane"), or paper impregnated with the semi-synthetic chemical ("blotter acid"). Tolerance builts up very rapidly but no withdrawal symptoms have been reported. A "trip" averages seven to eight hours, and the dosage is small compared to other drugs.

Physical effects include dilated pupils, flushed face, a feeling of being cold or hot, nausea, goose bumps, perspiration, increased blood sugar, and rapid heartbeat.

The psychological symptoms of LSD differ greatly depending on the personality of the user, the dosage, and the conditions under which the drug is taken. Symptoms can include loss of control over thought processes, feelings of invulnerability, anxiety, depression, breaks with reality, and sensations of enlightenment.

Vision can be markedly altered. People report changes in depth perception and in the meaning of what they see, as well as illusions and hallucinations. Their sense of time and of themselves is altered, and emotions range from bliss to horror.

The "flashback" is the best known although sometimes contested psychological effect of LSD. A flashback is a recurrence of some of the features of the LSD experience, days or even months after the last dose. Without warning, people flash back into their trips. These flashbacks can occur spontaneously, or can be prompted by use of antihistamines, marijuana, or by stimuli similar to those present during the trip.

PCP

PCP (phencyclidine) is a psychoactive substance that is currently very "in." It is usually inhaled via smoking on a tobacco or marijuana cigarette, or taken orally.

The psychological effects of PCP include disorientation, distortions of body image, vivid dreaming, and an inability to integrate or interpret sensory data that can lead to cataleptic states in some people.

Physical symptoms include difficulty in speaking, lack of muscle coordination, dizziness, drooping eyelids, rapid heartbeat, sweating, increased deep tendon reflexes, and involuntary eye movements. People usually have some hypertension and breathing irregularities. In the case of very large doses, there are convulsions and respiratory arrest.

The rapid and involuntary eye movements and mental dullness distinguish PCP from the hallucinogens. Because of its' powerful anesthetizing effects, PCP users may feel no pain, which

renders them exceedingly dangerous. If you suspect that someone has taken PCP, he should be put in a quiet room with as
few stimuli as possible and watched carefully. If you suspect an
overdose, get him to a hospital. Overdoses of PCP can be fatal.

Hallucinogens

Hallucinogens (peyote, mescaline, psilocybin, psilocyn, DOM,
DMT, DET, MDA,) are also called psychedelics. They bring
about changes in sensation, thinking, self-awareness, emotions,
and perceptions of time and space. People also experience illusions and delusions that may be minor or overwhelming, depending on the person and the dosage. The results vary each time
the drug is taken.

The best description I have found of hallucinogens is from
Drugs of Abuse, put out by the Department of Justice:

> The hallucinogenic drugs are substances, both natural and
> synthetic, that distort the perception of objective reality.
> They produce sensory illusions, making it difficult to
> distinguish between fact and fantasy. If taken in large
> doses, they cause hallucinations—the apparent percep-
> tion of unreal sights and sounds. Under the influence of
> hallucinogens, a user may speak of "seeing" sounds and
> "hearing" colors. His senses of direction, distance, and
> time become disoriented. Restlessness and sleeplessness
> are common until the drug wears off. Recurrent use pro-
> duces tolerance, inviting the use of greater amounts. The
> greatest hazard of the hallucinogens is that their effects
> are unpredictable each time they are taken. Toxic reac-
> tions that precipitate psychotic reactions and even death
> can occur. Persons in hallucinogenic states should be
> closely supervised—and upset as little as possible—to
> keep them from harming themselves and others. There

is no documented withdrawal syndrome. The hallucinogens have therefore not been shown to produce physical dependency.

MDA

"Ecstasy," the "Love Drug." Of all the hallucinogens, MDA and its derivative MDM are perhaps the most popular at this time. MDA is a synthetic compound derived from amphetamine, and known as 3, 4-methylenedioxyamphetamine. It is a white to gray-white powder that can be swallowed, inhaled, or injected. MDA produces a rush of exhilaration followed by several hours of euphoria and physical sensitivity. Paradoxically, users describe a state of both intense stimulation and intense relaxation, accompanied by mild hallucinations.

Drug Survival News (April 1982) says of MDA:

Devotees may depict MDA/MDM in glowing terms, but the drugs have also been linked with a number of serious side effects in users, generally tied to the intense levels of stimulation produced by their amphetamine base.

Primary among these effects is the danger of overdose triggered by gradual buildup of tolerance to the drug's amphetamine component. And even occasional use may produce physical and psychological burnout.

Cautioning that limited evidence makes it difficult to describe long-term effects of MDA/MDM use, [University of Oregon Drug Information Center counselor Jerome Beck] cites general deterioration of health and development of a severe psychological disorder similar to amphetamine psychosis as probable consequences of extended use. "We can really only take a case study and assume it will be amphetamine-like," Beck said. "But MDA and MDM are among the 'hardest' drugs we've

encountered.'' Even though there's limited medical research, from descriptions of people the day after . . . it
appears to be a very hard drug on the body.

Minor Tranquilizers.

The purpose of these depressant drugs (Librium, Valium, me-
probomate, Miltown, and others) is to control tension, anxiety,
headaches, gastrointestinal disturbances, insomnia, and emotional problems. Some of the short-term effects are that they
suppress brain centers, relax muscles, release inhibitions, slow
heart rate and metabolism, cause drowsiness, and lower blood
pressure.

In the long term, they can be addicting. Because they are
metabolized so slowly and remain in the body so long (sometimes days after they are taken), they are often unknowingly
combined with alcohol. When this happens, the effect of the
tranquilizer is increased, causing a ''double down,'' or additive
effect. The effect of Valium and alcohol is syngergistic, or multiple. The combination of tranquilizers and alcohol can cause coma
and death.

With minor tranquilizers, there is a tendency toward delayed withdrawal. This means that withdrawals may not start to
occur until several weeks after their use has been discontinued.
Abrupt cessation after prolonged periods of use can lead to serious mental disturbances and psychotic states.

Amphetamines and other stimulants.

In the past, amphetamines (Dexamyl, Dexadrine, Benzedrine,
methedrine, Preludin, Ritalin, ''speed,'' ''bennies,'' ''uppers''
and ''pep pills'') have been used to treat narcolepsy, to treat hyperactivity in children, and for controlled weight loss.

The short-term effects of these drugs are to stimulate the
central nervous system, increase breathing rate, cause dryness

of mouth and excessive perspiration, constrict blood vessels, reduce appetite, increase heart rate, raise blood pressure, dilate pupils, and cause restlessness and tremors.

The more serious or long-term effects are agitation, delusions, paranoia, feelings of grandeur, exhaustion, impairment of the liver, psychosis, severe depression, and blackouts.

Combined with alcohol, the effect of amphetamines is additive. Even more than with coffee, one simply becomes a more wide-awake and agitated drunk.

Tolerance to amphetamines tends to increase. More and more are needed to produce the same result. The withdrawal that follows takes the form of exhaustion and/or severe depression.

Barbiturates and other sedative hypnotics.
These include phenobarbital, rentobarbital, secobarbital, Seconal, Nembutal, Quaalude, Placidyl, Equanil, and others. They are known as "barbs," goofballs, blues, rainbows, reds, downers, ludes, soapers, etc. Their medical uses in the past have been for sedation, sleeping aid, anesthesia, lowering of blood pressure, and control of epilepsy.

In the short term, these drugs lower blood pressure, interfere with oxygen consumption in the brain, depress the heart, affect coordination, cause slurred speech, and reduce emotional control.

Their chronic use causes hyperactivity. The liver produces extra cells, causing the drug to metabolize faster and contributing cross-tolerances with other drugs, especially alcohol. This means that whatever tolerance the user has developed for the barbiturates, he has also developed for alcohol, and vice versa.

The drugs are highly addictive. Withdrawal is literally deadly and must be supervised medically.

Combined with alcohol, barbiturates are synergistic. The effect is "multiple." One drink plus one barbiturate does not equal two; it may equal four or six. Even small amounts of each, when combined, can lead to coma and death—witness Janis Joplin, Dorothy Kilgallen, Jimi Hendrix, and Judy Garland.

Cross-Tolerance: Many drug users develop cross tolerance. This means their increased tolerance to one drug creates an increased tolerance to many other drugs. For example, a heroin addict will need more alcohol to produce a high once his tolerance to heroin has developed.

ATTITUDES ABOUT ALCOHOL AND OTHER DRUGS

Ever since the temperance movement there has been a mystique of fear and guilt surrounding alcohol and other drugs in our country. Ask any group of people their opinions about alcohol and drugs, including grammar school children, and those answers will be mostly negative. Most small children are much more aware of destructive drinking behavior than their parents realize. Regardless of the fact that 70 percent of the U. S. population drinks alcohol at least on occasion, most groups I talk with tell me alcohol is unhealthy, a huge contributor to death and crime, the root of many family problems, costly to us as individuals and as a nation, and everyone would be better off without it. And most people don't realize their attitudes are so negative until we start talking about it.

What happens when your child goes out and has his first experience with alcohol? It may be terrible, but chances are, it'll be a pleasant experience. He'll be with his friends, feeling the euphoria and the strange new sensations in his body, and probably nothing worse will happen than a little hangover the next day. Now he thinks that everything he's decided about alcohol must be wrong. In addition, much of what he had heard about alcohol doesn't jibe with his experience. That creates conflict.

As if that weren't confusing enough, our society's negative

attitudes toward alcohol and other drugs result in a cachet attached to being able to "handle" them. This cachet is expressed in attitudes such as: "He can really drink like a man!" This perpetuates the idea that having a high tolerance to alcohol is a good thing, something to which you can attach your self-worth and even your sexual identity. In fact, tolerance is a symptom of alcoholism.

The myth of "the man who can hold his booze" makes a hero out of the guy who can chug down massive amounts of alcohol and not get drunk. These attitudes are harmful enough in the minds of adults, but in the minds of teenagers they often get exaggerated to the point where drinking becomes *seeing how much you can drink*. The kid who can chug a six-pack, walk a straight line, and drive everybody home may be considered more of a "responsible drinker" than the kid "losing his cookies" in the potted plants, but he may also be an incipient alcoholic. And what teenager is going to jeopardize his sexual identity by admitting he can't handle alcohol?

There has been more than one death reported in recent years resulting from college students forcing their peers or fraternity pledges to drink fatal doses of alcohol. By the time you're approaching the fatal dose, you're in no position to judge where you are or to stop it. Once a certain point is reached it's fairly easy to go over the line, especially when booze and marijuana (with its nausea reducing qualities) are combined.

The attitudes and myths seem to work in just the opposite way where girls are concerned. If a man is good at drinking a lot, a woman who does is bad. She'd better remain ladylike and do her drinking in the closet. Girls and women who get drunk are considered tramps, floozies, and cheap. They are accused of being promiscuous—and they sometimes are, because of the alcohol. That's not an excuse, it's just what happens. But peer pressure is exerted on girls, too, to be "one of the group" and yet to act like a lady.

One of the most damaging attitudes our society has is that, for some reason, we think people are funny when they act drunk. Dean Martin and Foster Brooks have made careers of imitating drunken slurs and staggers, and we've made them rich and famous for it. I daresay if they imitated slurs and staggers occurring as the result of a concussion or diabetic coma, no matter how funny they looked, no one would laugh.

No wonder that a young teenager soon concludes that whatever adults try to tell him about alcohol—whether they are teachers, counselors, parents, or coaches—is suspect. He has a new filter now: "Adults lie about alcohol." On the one hand, they drink it, laugh at it, admire heavy drinkers. On the other hand, they say it's bad. Having tried it, the kid likes it and enjoys having experience with so "charged" a substance. Now the battle is on. We feel powerless, worried, and in total reaction to what is going on.

This is the basic reason that communicating about alcohol and other drugs is so difficult, not only with children but with one another. We are usually in reaction when we talk about it. Our fears and attitudes get in the way of our responding to the situation at hand. We're thinking, "It's all over now. My son tried marijuana and it's only a matter of time before he's a heroin addict."

We think if our daughter tries cocaine, she'll be in jail within a week for pushing. We have to face the reality that these drugs are as available to our children as beer was to us, and that they may have to choose about them every time they go to a party.

COMMUNICATING WITH OUR KIDS ABOUT ALCOHOL AND OTHER DRUGS

In order to start communicating effectively about alcohol and other drugs, we have to take the charge off the issue. We have to know the facts and accept them. We have to be aware of when we are reacting and step back into response. Here are some typical ways in which the subject of alcohol comes up and how to handle them:

Joey is 10 years old. His mother, Celine, has noticed money missing from her purse. Her initial reaction is disbelief. Joey, her only child, wouldn't steal from her, and yet the evidence is growing stronger and stronger that he has done so.

One day Celine suspects she smells alcohol on Joey's breath. She is panicked. Her ex-husband is an alcoholic and the prospect of Joey becoming like him is just too much for her. What does she need to do?

First she must be clear about her own attitudes, or her hysteria will just drive Joey underground. Next she needs to observe her judgments. Calling Joey a thief and a drunk won't help anything. She also needs to clarify what Joey's drinking represents to her, which in this case is that he'll grow up to be like his dad.

A ten-year-old who has been stealing money and drinking beer is not apt to admit it. So Celine must communicate something that lets Joey know what she knows, without it being an accusation. She might say something like "When I was your age I used to take money from my mom's purse and buy candy bars. I was always afraid she knew, but I did it anyway. I really wanted those candy bars!" In other words, she should find something Joey can relate to, but she mustn't lie.

Then, a day or two later she might tell Joey her fears about alcohol, based on what she has observed. Something like, "Kids seem to be drinking alcohol earlier and earlier these days, Joey. It concerns me because of the damage alcohol can cause to the brain and liver of young people. Did you know alcohol kills brain cells?"

Joey will probably say "no" and that will be that, until a day or two later when Celine might ask, "Joey, have you ever drunk alcohol?"

Chances are Joey will still not talk—but he will be starting to think. At some level he knows he's being found out, but the communication is low pressure enough to keep him from feeling attacked. His mother's interest and concern are seeping through. As to her understanding of his position, chances are he may soon begin to enter into the conversation with information on what "his friends" are doing.

Celine has two major responsibilities at this point. One is to keep close track of the money in her purse, perhaps even keeping her purse out of sight. And the second is to keep gently presenting the subject of alcohol. This will seem exceedingly strange, however, if that's *all* she talks about. Her main purpose at this point is to keep communication open on all topics. If Joey's symptoms continue or escalate, Celine must confront him directly and set up consequences.

She might have to say, "Joey, I suspect you drink alcohol when you go over to Tom's house. I smell it on your breath when you come home—even when you sleep over. You're ten years old, Joey. I'm your mom and I'm responsible for your health. Alcohol is dangerous for a ten-year-old, so I'm going to have to keep you home for two months. At the end of that time I'll be willing to reconsider, as long as no incidents occur with alcohol between now and then."

What Celine is doing is taking responsibility. In a nonjudging, nonpunitive way she is responding to what she sees happening. She is willing to do her job as a parent, regardless of Joey's reactions. She is serving as a model for Joey by demonstrating that she doesn't have to be at Joey's mercy. Joey may be mad at her, but he's also learning that she can be trusted to support his well-being.

But what do we do with a teenager who has more independence and probably more money than Joey?

Helen is fifteen years old. She's a solid B student, is on the soccer team, and is class president. She is more outgoing than she used to be and is just this year becoming a member of the "in" group. Her father, Ed, is delighted to see her doing so well, both academically and socially.

One Friday evening Ed picks up Helen after a school dance. Ed has never smoked pot, but he's been to a few shindigs where others did, and he can't help but notice an odor when Helen, giggling, gets into the car. He looks at her red-rimmed eyes and that's all it takes. He knows the symptoms. He knows she's been smoking pot and he explodes. He's so angry he can barely drive the car. "What the hell have you been doing?" he yells. "You've been smoking pot, that's what! Your're grounded for a month. No daughter of mine is going to be a pothead."

Needless to say, stoned or not, Helen is terrified. She's never seen her father like this before. She's stopped giggling by now and is cowering in the corner of the car. She's also beginning to feel defiant. By the time he gets home, Ed realizes he's blown it.

But has he? Only if he decides to justify his anger, or try to pretend nothing has happened in hopes it will all blow away. Even though he went straight into reaction, it's not too late to respond.

The first thing Ed needs to do is to let Helen know what his reaction really meant. He can say, "I'm afraid that smoking pot means getting involved with the 'wrong people,' and that smoking pot means using harder drugs. I'm afraid you'll be harmed because not much is really known yet about the effects of marijuana and that means you'll lose everything you've worked so hard to gain." He might also let her know he, too, did things his parents would have feared, had they known about it.

Helen may stonewall him. She'll sigh, roll her eyes around, stare out the window, cross her arms, and swing her foot. Or she might yell, "What do you mean by the 'wrong people'? You think you know everything. Well, you don't!"

But Ed still needs to say what he has to say. It should be

short and to the point. Trying to get a response from her will drive him back into reaction. He needs to trust that his message is getting through because, at some level, it is.

If Helen does respond or react, Ed must be willing to hear her. If her reaction is defiance, withdrawal, or looking beaten (a surefire way to make dad feel guilty), Ed must watch his inclination to go back into reaction himself. Chances are he *will* react, but he needs to remember that he can react internally without dumping it on Helen.

Regardless of the success of the communication, if Ed feels a consequence is in order, he must stick to it. He can choose to modify the month's grounding, or keep it as is. The only thing he needs to do is see if his motive is punitive or if it is supportive. The consequence itself isn't the issue. The "ground of being"—the basic attitude—is what counts. If Ed chooses to follow through with the consequence, then he must be willing for Helen to go back into reaction. It is the natural thing for her to do. (Adults, when convicted in traffic court are no more receptive to the consequence than teens are to grounding.) But, at some level, if the communication lines are open, Helen will be able to receive her father's true intention—which is to support, love, and protect her.

Now, what if your child is absolutely refusing to respond—what might be going on? First of all, they may never have seen you really communicate before about anything touchy. That could make them suspicious right off the bat, so you must be patient.

Secondly, there's a payoff in no communication. If your parents really are able to duplicate your experience, you lose many of your excuses. Also, to a teen, duplication can seem like an intrusion.

Thirdly, defiance and resentment are tools for breaking away. Children who are totally delighted with their families have little motivation for moving on into the world. So let them have their reactions. They are normal and, to a certain degree, healthy and necessary. Just don't let their reactions be *your* excuse for not bothering to communicate.

SAYING NO

There has been a great deal written about saying "no" to alcohol, and most people agree that the way to do it is "any way you want." One of the best resources you can give your child is the knowledge that he has a right to say "no." He doesn't have to figure out "the best way" or figure out how he can refuse a proffered drink so everyone still likes him and approves of him—unless he wants to. "No, thank you" is all he needs to say. Some of the options to drinking, suggested in a current TV commercial for people who don't want to say just, "No, thank you" are:

"I'm driving."
"I'm drinking cola."
"I'm full."
"I have an early day tomorrow," or
"I have a test tomorrow."
"It doesn't agree with me."
"I'd rather dance."
"I'm allergic to it. It makes me break out
in bad judgment."

He doesn't have to be righteous about it. In fact, he probably doesn't want to or need to. It's a lot more acceptable now for adults to say they just don't want a drink than it was ten or twenty years ago. Let's make that option available to our children. Let your teenager practice saying "no" to you. People have more respect for others who know what they want and go after it—or who know what they don't want and stay away from it.

SEVEN

Alcoholism and Addiction

ALCOHOLISM IS A DISEASE

The first man in this century to shed light on alcoholism as a disease was Dr. E. M. Jellinek. Prior to his work in the 1940s, most people thought of alcoholism as a moral issue having more to do with sin and weakness than with illness. Dr. Jellinek's work played a leading role in turning America around about alcoholism and diminishing the stigma attached to it.

Jellinek was not an alcoholic himself, which is interesting because people generally think only alcoholics believe that alcoholism is a disease. Not only did Jellinek point out that it was a disease, but he described the different phases and symptoms and even formulated five different categories of alcoholism. He called them alpha, beta, gamma, delta, and epsilon. It's not important what each of them meant; the point is that he broke down the assumption that anyone with a drinking problem was an alcoholic and could be lumped into one overall category.

The American Medical Association first classified alcoholism as a disease in 1957; not a mental or social disease indicating weak-willed people who couldn't cope, but a physical disease. Alcoholism can't be cured, but it can be arrested if the alcoholic is willing to stop drinking.

The myths and misconceptions about alcoholism are as deep and widespread as those about alcohol. Even intelligent, well-informed people have misunderstandings about alcoholism. The purpose of this chapter is to clear up some of those misconceptions, present accurate information and, to the extent that I can, lessen the charge surrounding the issue of alcoholism.

Let's look first at exactly what alcoholism is. The following definition was developed by the National Council on Alcoholism and the American Medical Society's Alcoholism Committee on Definitions. It's long, but it's an accurate statement of what alcoholism is and presents a clear picture of the disease.

> Alcoholism is a chronic, progressive, and potentially fatal disease. It is characterized by: tolerance, physical dependency, and/or pathological organ changes all of which are the direct or indirect consequences of the alcohol ingested.
>
> 1. By chronic and progressive it is meant that there are both physical and emotional/social changes which are cumulative and progressive with the continuation of drinking.
>
> 2. By tolerance is meant body and brain adaptation to the presence of high concentrations of alcohol.
>
> 3. By physical dependency is meant that there are withdrawal symptoms upon decreasing or ceasing consumption of alcohol.
>
> 4. In addition, the individual with alcoholism cannot consistently predict on any drinking occasion the duration of the episode or the quantity which will be consumed.
>
> 5. Pathological organ changes can be found in almost any organ, but most often involve the liver, brain, peripheral nervous system, and the gastrointestinal tract.

6. The drinking pattern is generally continuous but may be intermittent with periods of abstinence between drinking episodes.

7. The *social, emotional, and behavioral symptoms and consequences result* from the *effect of alcohol* on the *function of the brain*. The degree to which these symptoms and signs are considered deviant will depend upon the cultural norms of the society or group in which the individual operates.

HEREDITARY DISEASE

There is a growing body of research suggesting that alcoholism is a hereditary disease. The hereditary factor isn't limited just to alcohol. Many authorities now believe that many other addictions, including those to Valium and other drugs, are caused by hereditary factors.

Some of the leading research in this area has been done by Dr. Donald Goodwin. He found that the sons of alcoholics were about four times as likely to be alcoholic as were the sons of nonalcoholics, even if the sons of the alcoholics had no exposure to their biological parents after the first few weeks of life. The intriguing part of his research, that most strongly suggests that alcoholism is a hereditary disease, is the finding that the sons of alcoholics were no more likely to become simply "heavy" or "problem" drinkers (but non-addicted) than were the sons of nonalcoholics.

This means that what was inherited was not the tendency to drink, but the disease of alcoholism. In order to be classified "alcoholic" in his study, the men not only had to drink excessively, but to experience severe alcohol-related living problems such as marital troubles and frequent blackouts.

Dr. Goodwin also compared adopted sons of alcoholics with their brothers who had been raised by the biological parents. He found that the rates of alcoholism of the two groups were almost the same, despite their different environments and upbringings. This finding causes some serious questions about the environmental factor as a cause of alcoholism

In his book based on these studies, *Is Alcoholism Hereditary?*, Dr. Goodwin concludes that his findings "tend to contradict the oft-repeated assertion that alcoholism results from the interaction of multiple causes—social, psychological, biological. This may be true of milder forms of alcoholism, but conceivably severe alcoholism could be relatively uninfluenced by environment, given free access to alcohol. The 'father's sins' may be visited on the sons even in the father's absence." And of course, alcoholism is no more a sin than is diabetes.

Further research showed that the likelihood of developing alcoholism was not increased by living with alcoholic parents, whether they were biological parents or stepparents. *The only consistent predictor of alcoholism was having an alcoholic biological parent.*

Dr. Michael Bohman, of the University of Umea in Sweden, studied 2,000 adoptees and their biological and adoptive parents. He found out that the adopted sons of alcoholics were about three times as likely to be alcoholics as were the adopted sons of nonalcoholics.

Another Swedish study compared identical twins (from a single egg, therefore with the same genetic structure) with fraternal twins (from two eggs, with different genetic structure), and found that both members of an identical twin set were twice as likely as the members of fraternal twin sets to evidence alcoholism. An American study examined the rates of alcohol metabolism and found that identical twins had the same metabolism, but that fraternal twins had different metabolisms. Both studies concluded that genetics played a larger role than environment in alcoholism.

These kinds of studies make a very strong case for the hereditary factor. Dr. Gian Salmioraghi, of the National Institute on Alcohol Abuse and Alcoholism, has said, "There are all sorts of theories. But there is a difference between theories and facts, and genetic studies are finally providing facts.'' He added, ''The findings we have in genetics are the most convincing we have for any of the theories as to the etiology (cause) of some forms of alcoholism.''

Genetic research has become the focus of a great deal more time, money, and attention as the evidence mounts that alcoholism is, indeed, a hereditary disease. Dr. Goodwin has said that this evidence is so strong that we should stop trying to figure out *whether* alcoholism is hereditary, and try to find out *what* is being transmitted that gives the children of alcoholics a tendency toward the disease.

''The evidence in the last ten years, of susceptibility to alcoholism that is independent of exposure to alcoholism in the environment, has become so good that it's time people started thinking about what is being transmitted,'' he says. ''What we need to do at this point is to study alcohol's effect on the brain more—see what it does, and then what you can do to block its action.''

Science magazine reported a study done at the University of Washington in Seattle. Twenty healthy young men with a history of alcoholism in their families, and a similar group with no history of alcoholism in their families, drank equal amounts of ethanol mixed with sugar-free Seven-Up. They took a series of blood samples to determine any variation in how each group's bodies broke down and used the alcohol.

The men with alcoholism in their families were more likely to have higher levels of a breakdown product called acetaldehyde. Increased acetaldehyde is known to enhance the state of intoxication and may predispose people to physiological damage from drinking. Abnormal acetaldehyde levels may be the metabolic marker for a genetic predisposition to alcoholism, but its connection to the mechanism of becoming an alcoholic is still a mystery.

Even ten years ago, the idea that one's genetic makeup pre-

disposed one toward alcoholism was often dismissed as hog-
wash. Today, it's crossed the border into scientific respectabil-
ity. In fact, it's the best idea we have. It's becoming fairly
generally accepted that alcoholics are born, not made.

BERNICE AND GERTRUDE

This is a story I tell children in the grammar schools to make
the point that alcoholism is a disease that some people get and
some don't. Before I tell the story of Bernice and Gertrude, I
talk about how everyone looks different, and has different kinds
of ideas and feelings. Sometimes the differences among people
can't be seen on the outside. Some people, for instance, are allergic to cats or to chocolate or to milk. Others aren't, but you
can't tell which is which just by looking at them. Then I tell the
story of Bernice and Gertrude, to show how some people develop alcoholism and some do not.

Bernice and Gertrude are the best of friends. One day they are
both invited to a friend's birthday party and, of course, they are
very excited to be going. When they get to the party, they discover that their hostess just loves chocolate. In fact, she loves it
so much that everything at the party is chocolate: chocolate cake,
chocolate ice cream, chocolate candy, even chocolate milk.
    They both eat a lot and when Bernice gets home a funny
thing happens. She starts to break out in red spots. When Gertrude gets home she has a bit of a tummy ache because she ate
so much, but she doesn't break out in red spots. Bernice shows
her mom the spots and her mom takes her to the doctor and he
tells her she is allergic to chocolate and shouldn't eat it anymore. Bernice feels horrible because she loves chocolate, but there
isn't much she can do about being allergic to it.
    About a month later, Bernice and Gertrude are invited to
another birthday party, but this time their hostess loves straw-

berries. Bernice is glad because there isn't anything chocolate to eat. It's all strawberry. There's strawberry cake, strawberry ice cream, strawberry milk, even fresh strawberries. Both Bernice and Gertrude eat lots of everything and go home with very full tummies. And again, Bernice breaks out in red spots. Her mom takes her to the doctor and she finds out she's allergic to strawberries, too. Now she can't eat her two favorite things—chocolate and strawberries!

Bernice and Gertrude grow up and go to the same college and remain the best of friends. In fact, they even weigh the same, 120 pounds. And they still go to parties together. One night they are at a party where alcohol is being served, so they both decide to have a drink. After her first drink, Bernice says to herself, "For heavens sake! This is amazing. I feel normal. I feel like this is how I always should have felt. My, this is good stuff. I think I'll have some more!" Gertrude starts to feel a little "happy." In a very short time, maybe ten minutes, both Bernice and Gertrude have a second drink. Bernice now feels even more "normal." Her vocabulary gets better; she's using words she didn't even know she knew. She doesn't feel shy. She can dance better. She feels more like herself than ever before! Gertrude, however, starts feeling a little silly. In fact, everything seems so funny to her that she's laughing all the time.

Bernice thinks, "Well, if this stuff works so well, maybe I'll have another drink." So Bernice takes a third drink and, since Gertrude and Bernice do everything together, Gertrude decides to have a third drink, too. Now Bernice goes off to talk to her biology professor with whom she has a very intelligent conversation, and Gertrude is laughing so hard she's crying. In fact, Gertrude is beginning to feel dizzy and is having a hard time standing up. Bernice decides to have a fourth drink, so of course Gertrude does, too. Now Bernice is starting to feel just a little giggly. But Gertrude can hardly stand up anymore. She is acting very silly and keeps tripping all over everyone.

Now who is having the unusual reaction to alcohol—Bernice or Gertrude?

At this point, a lot of the children say that Gertrude is having the unusual reaction, but some are perceptive enough to see that it is Bernice. Gertrude is acting drunk, but both she and Bernice are intoxicated. They both have the same amount of toxic substance in them.

But Bernice has a high tolerance, meaning that she can drink more alcohol without acting drunk. In fact, in the early stages of alcoholism, many alcoholics actually do function better than normal with some alcohol in their system. This is not really surprising when you realize that in the late stages, an unrecovered and undetoxified alcoholic can *only* function with alcohol in their body. Bernice was delighted at first when she found a substance to which she reacted so well, but actually the very fact that she had such a high tolerance to alcohol indicated that she might have the disease called alcoholism—that she might be "allergic" to alcohol.

MISCONCEPTIONS AND FACTS

Perhaps no other disease is surrounded by as many misconceptions as alcoholism, even among people who consider themselves well-informed. Our confusion about alcoholism, and the conflicts that confusion generates, are among the reasons we have been so ineffective as a society in dealing with it. These are some of the common misconceptions and the facts that relate to them. When you begin to inform your kids about alcoholism, one of the first things you may have to do is clear up some misconceptinns they may already have received from their peers—or even from you!

Misconception: Alcoholics are bums, jobless, homeless, incompetent, weak-willed people who live on skid row.

Fact: Only 3 to 5 percent of this country's ten million alcoholics fit this stereotype; 95 percent are employed or employable. They make up 5 percent of the work force and 10 percent of the executives in America.

Most alcoholics live with their families, in respectable neighborhoods. They are housewives, bankers, doctors, lawyers, farmers, salespeople, teachers, clergy, and just about any occupation you can imagine. They do normal things like going to baseball games and walking their dogs.

This stereotyped misconception prevents many people from recognizing that they are alcoholic, or that someone they love is alcoholic. They say, "Well, look. He got up and went to work this morning". Or, "But he's so clean and dresses so nicely. He has such a good job and he plays catch with his son!" Baloney! *Anyone can be an alcoholic.* The disease is completely nondiscriminatory about religion, age, economic background, status, sex, creed, or anything else. The answer to the question, "What kinds of people become alcoholics?" is *"All kinds."*

Misconception: Alcoholics are abnormal people with something wrong with them. There's something sinister and evil about them.

Fact: Alcoholics are just like other people, with all the same shining qualities, eccentricities, and problems—except that they can't drink alcohol without eventually losing control of their lives.

Once the disease has started, the situation is compounded by physical, emotional, and societal pressures. Sometimes their lives look chaotic, but basically they are ordinary human beings. Some people become violent when they drink, and some become withdrawn. That's just how the substance affects that particular person. It's not that an alcoholic does this and the rest of the world does that. It's true that if you look at alcoholics who are still drinking, you see some similarities. That's not because they're all alike, but because the drug alcohol has specific effects on any physical body.

Researchers have tried to find psychological differences between non-alcoholics and alcoholics who have been sober for two years, and they came up with absolutely nothing. Some are psychotic just like the rest of the folks. Some are creative, some are not. Some are bright, some are not so bright. They're just as neurotic as the rest of the population, but no more so.

Misconception: If you're an alcoholic, you discover it pretty soon after you start drinking. And you have to drink a lot to be an alcoholic.

Fact: Alcoholism can be triggered in twenty minutes, or in twenty years, after your first drink.

Many alcoholics have drunk very little, but their systems are not able to handle even that minimal amount. For them, two beers a week produce the same result as five Scotches a night might for another person. If the predisposition is there, it can get triggered at any time. In that respect, alcoholism is a little like diabetes. Sometimes they discover it in a young child, or a person becomes diabetic at age seventy. The potential can be there all along, but not manifest itself until late in life.

Misconception: Alcoholics know they're alcoholic. They just don't want to stop drinking, so they won't admit it.

Fact: Alcoholics rarely recognize themselves because of their stereotyped misconception. More than anyone, *they* are the people who think that alcoholics live on skid row, have no jobs, are always in and out of hospitals, have no self-discipline, beat their children, drink in the morning, and can't stop drinking any time they take a drink. Actually, a lot of these symptoms manifest themselves only in the later stages of alcoholism. Some alcoholics have some of them, and some have very few. Anyone who doesn't fit this stereotype, however, is apt to figure they *couldn't* be an alcoholic.

Misconception: If alcoholics could be made to see all the trouble they're causing, they'd stop drinking.

Fact: Alcoholics seldom connect their drinking to problems in their lives or in the lives of those they love.

The reason they don't stop drinking is that their bodies demand alcohol. In the beginning, this isn't the case. Their bodies don't *always* demand alcohol, so they *appear* to be able to drink in a social and controlled way.

Episodes of loss of control are often few and far between, and are thought of as simply "sowing wild oats," or an "occasional drunk." But suggest that the person stop drinking altogether, and watch the reaction. Any reaction that vehement must come from a position of protection. The alcoholic's body is demanding to be protected from giving up alcohol.

Misconception: Since the alcoholic's body demands alcohol, it's hopeless to think an alcoholic can stop drinking.

Fact: Alcoholics can stop drinking, just as diabetics can stop eating sugar. It isn't always easy, however.

The attitudes of the people around the alcoholic make a big difference in the alcoholic's willingness to get sober and stay sober. A diabetic isn't told that "one bit of sugar won't hurt you," or that "you're not really a diabetic," or "if you had will power you could control your blood sugar." These are the kinds of things alcoholics hear all the time about their drinking.

Misconception: Alcoholics are emotionally disturbed.

Fact: Alcohol upsets the entire body chemistry, creating anxiety, depression, and hallucinations.

When alcoholics are under the influence or in withdrawal, they are apt to do some very strange things. These disturbances are caused by the alcohol. Once the alcohol is removed from the body and the chemistry returns to normal, alcoholics show no greater signs of emotional disturbance than the rest of the population.

Misconception: All alcoholics will eventually end up on skid row.

Fact: Very few alcoholics live long enough to wind up on skid row.

On the average, alcoholics die ten years earlier than the general population. Their death certificates seldom read, "Cause of death: alcoholism." They usually say, "Hemorrhagic ulcer," or "Gastritis," or "Pancreatitis," or "Cirrhosis," or "Heart failure." Some alcoholics end up in mental institutions, some live in a "fog" until they die at ninety-two, and quite a few recover from the disease and live without drinking.

Misconception: Alcoholics cannot be helped until they ask for it.

Fact: The majority of alcoholics don't even know they're alcoholic, so why should they ask for help?

If you want an alcoholic to get help, learn how to communicate with him. What looks like help usually isn't. Alcoholics can be helped, but only if the person helping knows what he's doing.

Misconception: The main reason alcoholics don't quit drinking is because they can't live without alcohol.

Fact: The main reason alcoholics don't quit drinking is because they don't realize they are alcoholic.

The stigma around alcoholism makes it difficult for people to recognize their illness, much less recover from it. No one wants to admit they're weak-willed, irresponsible, uncontrolled, with massive personality disorders—yet that is society's point of view about alcoholics. Can you blame them for not wanting to admit that? When society truly understands alcoholism, it will become a lot easier for alcoholics to acknowledge their disease and to recover from it.

Misconception: People with a high tolerance to alcohol are lucky. They never get drunk, or get hangovers.

Fact: They may, however, be alcoholic. One of the earliest symptoms of alcoholism is high tolerance.

Misconception: People with a low tolerance cannot be alcoholic.

Fact: Alcoholism doesn't depend on drinking a certain amount of alcohol. It's what happens when you drink that's important.

Misconception: A man who is fifty, never misses a day of work, and drinks only on weekends couldn't be an alcoholic.

Fact: Yes he could.

What happens when he drinks? Is it affecting his health? Family life? Work? Social life? General well-being? That's the issue. Is he controlling it or is it controlling him?

Misconception: Getting drunk occasionally is to be expected. It's nothing to worry about. Everyone does it.

Fact: Getting drunk only once can be enough to create problems.

Just one auto accident is all you need to change your life permanently. Continued episodes of getting drunk can be early symptoms of alcoholism, or can trigger alcoholism in those who are predisposed to it. Getting drunk is never safe.

The truth is, 30 percent of the adult population does not drink at all, and only 20 percent of the remaining 70 percent who drink ever get drunk. Getting drunk, in this case, means "out of control." It doesn't mean "high," which is happy but not sloppy.

In countries where getting drunk is not condoned, alcoholism rates are low, perhaps because the people are less likely to drink enough at any one time to trigger the disease.

Misconception: It's the person's own fault if he becomes alcoholic. He did it to himself.

Fact: As we've recently learned, alcoholism is a physical disease with possible hereditary factors.

A PROBLEM DRINKER VERSUS AN ALCOHOLIC

It's no news to anyone that a lot of drinking goes on between the ages of sixteen to twenty-five. That's when people are sowing their wild oats, experimenting, and rebelling. And that's when a lot of people also develop drinking problems; not necessarily alcoholism, but drinking problems.

They might get arrested a few times for drunk driving, or have a couple of unpleasant incidents and lots of headaches. Somewhere at the ages of twenty-three to twenty-six, or even in their late twenties, they'll figure that the kicks they get from drinking don't make up for the possible dangers and the horrible headaches and they'll say, "Forget this"!

They'll become light or moderate drinkers, or their doctor will tell them to take it easy with the booze, and they do. The difference between them and an alcoholic is that they can cut down on the amount they drink—forever.

Alcoholics can't do that for any lengthy period of time (six months or more). Let me make this clear now: Alcoholics can *stop* drinking. What they can't do consistently for long periods or in the later stages, is simply cut down. They keep right on drinking in a way that is detrimental to their physical, emotional, spiritual, and social well-being. They are the victims of alcoholism.

If your child is a problem drinker, he or she can and will cut down on the amount and consequences if you are clear and firm in your expectations. An alcoholic child will be unable to control his drinking or the consequences over a period of six months to a year. Regardless of the reasons, if your child does not control his drinking, you must get professional help.

HOW ALCOHOLISM DEVELOPS

Alcoholism is a progressive disease. It develops over a period of time, and gets worse as the person continues to drink and to age. By the time a person has come to resemble what we generally think of as an alcoholic—"disgusting, abusive, destructive, defiant, fearful, resentful, angry, lonely, scared, arrogant, inconsistent, frightful, drunk in the morning, bums, winos, crazy, mean, dizzy, violent, vegetable-like"*—they're very far along in the illness.

Progressive diseases are often hard to identify in their early stages. In this respect, alcoholism is similar to heart disease. When does heart disease start? When somebody has trouble walking up the stairs? When they have their first pain in the chest? Their third? When they start having high cholesterol? When they have a heart attack? It's hard to say. The same is true of alcoholism. By the time you say, "I think he's turning into an alcoholic," he already *is* one and has been for some time.

The following are some of the general symptoms of alcoholism in the early, middle and later stages. They are meant to provide an overview, not to be interpreted rigidly or used to make a case against anybody. In the next chapter we'll look at how these stages might be manifested in teenagers.

*Taken from a list made up by adults when asked to describe the characteristics of alcoholics

EARLY STAGES

1. Increased tolerance (may be innate and then built up through repeated ingestion of the substance coupled with the experience of needing increasingly more to produce the desired result).
2. Personality changes.
3. Occasional undesired consequences when drunk or hung over.
4. Increasing dependence on or interest in activities involving alcohol. Loves ball games, parties, dinner with wine; hates parties without alcohol or other drugs, the theater (but loves intermission if drinks are served!).
5. Sometimes no drinking for days, weeks, or months; but loss of control when drinking occurs. Often loss of control happens on only one of five or ten drinking occasions—which is "proof" there is no problem.
6. Surrounding yourself with others who drink as much as or more than you do, so you don't stand out in the crowd.
7. Memory loss (blackout or brownout).
8. Relief drinking (in reaction to quarrels, pressure, etc.).
9. Discomfort in certain situations without alcohol.
10. Drinking beyond your intentions.
11. Occasionally missing work or school, especially on Mondays or following holidays.

MIDDLE STAGES

1. Gulping drinks, hurrying to get the first one down.
2. Sneaking drinks (between rounds, before a party).
3. Drinking at the same time daily.
4. Beginnings of denial (guilt feelings, not happy to discuss drinking, lying about it, finding excuses and causes, irritability, self-righteousness).
5. Loss of control, not only of "how much" but "when."

6. Promises to stop (to self or others).
7. Manipulating circumstances to try and control problem (going "on the wagon" for six months, or a week; switching brands; switching to beer or wine; changing jobs or cities).
8. Remorse (over what you did or said).
9. Absenteeism on or off the job (job or school performance deteriorates).

LATE STAGES

1. Addiction ("the shakes," other withdrawal symptoms).
2. Preoccupation with alcohol (protecting the stash, not letting other activities interfere with your drinking).
3. Avoidance of family and friends while drinking (loneliness).
4. Paranoia ("nobody understands," "they're unfair").
5. Binge drinking.
6. Decrease in tolerance.
7. Depression, unreasonable fears, delirium tremens.
8. Physical illness associated with alcohol (liver or nervous system damage; ulcers or intestinal bleeding, malnutrition).

I want to stress that these symptoms are only guidelines, not hard and fast rules. They are the standards some people use, but having one of these symptoms doesn't necessarily mean you're an alcoholic—although you can be an alcoholic with very few of them. Most early-stage alcoholics will recognize none of these symptoms. They have rationalizations for the way they drink, which is the first indication that they are in the process of denial. As with heart disease, it's difficult to tell when alcoholism begins. Is it when people start drinking in the morning? When they crave a drink at a particular time of day? When they begin to take bigger and taller drinks? When their tolerance goes up dramatically? Or when it goes down? When their bodies only feel "normal" after a drink?

Most alcoholics start out being controlled or social drinkers. For some people, that controlled drinking can last for twenty years. For others, it lasts twenty minutes. Alcoholism begins in different people at different times, and we don't yet know how or why it happens. Some people build up a tolerance to five to seven drinks a day, and can do that forever without becoming alcoholics.

Such people may suffer some physical damage, but if their doctor tells them to cut down, it's no problem for them to do so. It doesn't really change their lives substantially at all. People used to say, "If you drink too much, you'll become an alcoholic." The truth is, we have no idea what "too much" is. We only know that it varies from person to person, and that whatever point at which you lose control, that is too much. The problem is that you don't know until after the fact that you drank enough to trigger the alcoholism.

The operative principle with alcoholics is that we will drink as much as we need to drink in order to produce the result we want. That result is actually physiological, but it is experienced as psychological. It's experienced as going from feeling abnormal to feeling normal. In this case, psychological and physiological feel like the same thing.

For me one drink might make the difference in how I experience myself. All I want is to get from here to there, from point A to point B. If one drink will do it, fine. But if it takes throwing up five drinks before I can keep enough alcohol down long enough to get there, that's what I'll do if I'm an alcoholic.

PROGRESSION

Usually, our tolerance builds until we have our first negative incident. Maybe it's getting drunk and doing something out of character like getting into a screaming match with a friend. Maybe it's not being able to make it to school on Monday morning, or having a blackout. Something happens that's detrimental, out of character, and related to our "social drinking."

After that first incident, we're likely to cut back for a while. The cutting back is successful, so after a while our mind says, "Hey, there's no problem here! I'm not getting into any trouble! Let's have a drink!"

So, usually unconsciously, we go back to drinking as much as before, or more, and our tolerance continues to increase. Before you know it, we have our next incident. Maybe this time we have a car accident. We cut back again. It starts to look like this:

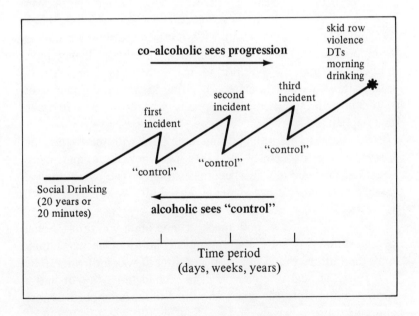

Someone looking at us from the outside, says, "Here is a person headed for death and destruction." But all we see is, "I still don't drink in the morning." "I can still drink the way I used to." The denial has started. The more someone tries to convince us that we have a problem, the more we resist. Can you see how the communication problems get started?

As the body becomes addicted to the substance, it begins to require alcohol in order to feel normal. Many alcoholics have shared the experience of taking their first drink and saying to themselves, "So *this* is what I've been missing. So this is how a human being is supposed to feel!" This is the very first drink of their lives, and immediately they know what they've been missing. *That's not normal.* It's an abnormal reaction to the substance, but it's quite a common experience. It's as if this body and that substance were made for each other, and they both know it. Amazing how the whole thing backfires!

Even if it didn't start out that way, however, the body craves alcohol to feel normal once the addiction has started to take hold. When alcoholics crave a drink, it's not because they are having an emotional reaction. The craving is in their body. If they have to create a "reason," an upset to justify the drink, they will. In a stressful situation, the person is going to want more than ever to feel normal, and there's only one way he knows how to make that happen.

So, as these incidents pile up—the fight with the friend, the blackout, the car crash—and life becomes more and more stressful, the need to drink becomes stronger. The psychological and the physiological factors get all mixed up. We can't tell which is which.

It's not a matter of how much or how often you drink. Some people drink very little and yet are alcoholics. One man drank only three times in his life, but each time it was a disaster. The first time, he beat up his wife. The second time, he got into a serious automobile accident. The third time, he robbed a store and ended up in prison. He saw that his life was totally out of control when he drank, and started with AA while in prison. It didn't matter that he only drank on three occasions; what mattered was that his life was out of control because of alcohol. He realized he was an alcoholic.

Some alcoholics never do build up a high tolerance. They can't control their behavior even after one or two drinks. The thing that makes alcoholism so difficult to recognize in ourselves is denial: we go to the lists of symptoms and check off the ones we *don't* have, rather than the ones we do. We forget that alcoholism manifests itself differently in everyone, and that the person who has two drinks and is frequently out of control is just as much an alcoholic as the person who has fifteen drinks and still looks pretty straight. The evidence isn't on the list; it's in our lives.

The major symptom of alcoholism is loss of control. That doesn't mean always drinking uncontrollably. Loss of control can be gradual. We might start out with a 2 percent loss of control; 98 percent of the time we appear to be in control. Then 20 percent of the time we're out of control and 80 percent seems controlled. Then it starts moving up to 30/70, then 50/50, then 60/40, etc. There are all kinds of excuses, like being tired or not having had enough to eat. The fact remains, however, that *if we are losing control, we've lost control.*

If we profess that we can always control our drinking and drink two drinks for five nights in a row, but then get smashed on the sixth night when we didn't intend to, we're out of control. It never seems that way to the alcoholic. He will always say, "I'm tired; I deserve it." "I had a fight with my wife." "I missed my train." But the truth is, his drinking is out of control. A controlled drinker can limit the amount and the consequences at will. No excuses or justifications are necessary. An alcoholic needs excuses because he doesn't understand why he can't control his drinking.

THE DOWN SIDE

There comes a time when the tolerance stops increasing and starts to drop dramatically. Since this usually takes many years of heavy drinking it does not often appear in teenagers, though there are exceptions. It can happen very suddenly. One night, the guy who used to drink eleven double martinis with no problems can barely stand up after two martinis.

He'll probably think he was coming down with the flu, or ate the wrong thing. The next time he goes out drinking, he'll have nine double martinis and everything will be fine. "See?" he'll say, "There was nothing to worry about after all."

But then a week later, he'll go out and have two martinis and get roaring drunk. Then next week he'll go out and have seven and be okay. It starts to look like this:

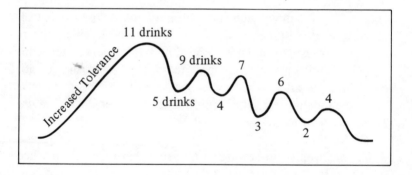

It scares the alcoholic to watch his tolerance drop. And again, the communication suffers. The person who's around the alcoholic will see the times when he has one drink and is on his ear. The alcoholic will see only the time he had nine and was fine.

Tolerance diminishes further until finally, he doesn't even have to worry about tolerance anymore. His liver has deteriorated to the point that the alcohol is circulating freely in his system. One drink will do it because the alcohol remains for hours. The person has a constant "buzz."

The next step is that there is no "buzz" anymore, no matter how much he drinks. No amount of alcohol brings the feeling back. That would be a great time to quit. But the alcoholic doesn't always see it that way. Often he'll keep trying.

MEDICINE STORY

The following is a story which illustrates how the disease of alcoholism can progress. It's a simple illustration of the principles involved, told in terms children can understand and identify with. You might want to share it with your younger children.

Let's suppose that you and your sister Nancy are both sick and your mom gives you both a spoonful of medicine. The medicine doesn't change the way Nancy feels, but somehow, it makes you feel more like yourself than you usually do. It makes you feel especially good inside— peaceful, warm, and cozy.

The next time you both get sick, you're glad—it means you can have some more medicine. But one spoonful doesn't make you feel better this time. You have to have two spoonfuls. Nancy is glad she just has to have one, because the medicine doesn't make her feel as good as it makes you feel. You feel great now that you've had two spoonfuls.

Then one day you don't feel very energetic or happy, not like yourself, and you remember that there's something that makes you feel better. The medicine! You think about taking some, but you know that you're never supposed to take medicine without a grownup giving it to you, so you don't have any. But you think about it a lot.

Years later, when you're old enough to take medicine without a grown-up giving it to you, you get sick and you take the medicine. It makes you feel very good, just as it did when you were little. Now, if you have something that makes you feel more like yourself, what might you want to do? Right. Take it a lot. And take a lot *of* it. So sometimes you might take the medication even when you're not sick, just when you want to feel better. Nancy thinks you're crazy. She doesn't see that it has a different effect on you than it does on her.

Pretty soon, you notice you feel a little funny when you're *not* taking the medicine. You begin to think that the medicine is the only way to feel normal, and you just don't feel very good unless you take it. You don't realize that it's because of the medicine that you feel bad, so you just keep taking more. It used to be that two spoonfuls made you feel better, but now it takes four or six. Before long, your body feels as though it needs the medicine.

So let's imagine that you've been taking the medicine every time you feel bad for many years.—so many years that you're grown up and have your own apartment. Now you have your own money, so you have *cabinets* full of the medicine. And instead of taking spoonfuls, now you drink the medicine out of a glass. Sometimes when you don't take it your body gets sick and shaky and you're always forgetting things. But you know the medicine is the only thing that's going to make you feel better.

Then one day, just as you're sitting down to pour yourself a nice big glass of medicine, I walk in and say, "Give me that medicine! It's making you sick!" I come over and start to take the medicine away from you, but you fight me for it because you think, "It isn't making me sick; it's making me better!"

Then I say, "I'm going to take all your bottles of medicine and pour them down the sink!" What might you do? Well, you might start hiding them so I couldn't find them. You might scream at me, "You don't understand! The medicine's making me better!" You'd try to keep me from taking it from you. The more I tried to take it away from you, the more upset you'd get.

Now the truth is that the medicine isn't making you better; it's been making you worse. But are you bad for wanting the medicine? No, it's just that it makes you sick. It didn't make Nancy sick, but you had a different reaction to the medicine than she did. And the trouble is, you *thought* it made you feel better.

The same thing happens to people who have the sickness of alcoholism. They have different reactions to alcohol than other people. It makes them sick. They aren't bad for being sick, but if they want to get better they have to go on a diet. A nonalcohol diet.

DENIAL

Alcoholism is a disease of denial, which means that people don't want to admit that they have it. The alcoholic refuses to see that he's an alcoholic. In many cases, so does his family, so they reinforce one another. Because of the added stigma suffered by alcoholic women, in their case the denial is even greater.

Like some forms of cancer, alcoholism has periods of remission, periods when the drinking seems to be under control. At those times, it's easy to deny that the illness is there and that it is going to manifest itself again. In this respect, alcoholism is no different from any other disease in which denial operates. When my father got an incurable form of cancer, I found myself denying it. Dad had lymphoma; a tumor was pressing against his sciatic nerve. When they cut the nerve and he was free of most of the pain and just limped a little, I convinced myself that everything was going to be all right. I heaved a great sigh of relief and almost believed that he didn't have cancer anymore. But my denial didn't help me or anyone else, in the long run.

Many chronic diseases provoke denial. Some diabetics don't take their insulin, and they eat large amounts of carbohydrates or sugars. A friend who works in a diabetic ward tells me they have to lock the patients in because they keep sneaking out to the candy machine.

Heart disease can be the same way. Doctors have a terrible time treating people who have high blood pressure. The patients don't feel it, so in their minds, they simply don't have it. Why should they take their pills? They don't have any symptoms.

Well, alcoholics don't feel anything either. In addition to being too close to it to see it, and not wanting to see it, they're physically anesthetized! The anesthesia compounds and perpetuates the denial. How can they look? They're "under" half the time, and feeling no pain.

Denial is one of five steps in a paradigm used by Dr. Elizabeth Kubler-Ross in her work with dying patients. Not everyone goes through each step, in the same order or at any predictable pace. Her framework is valuable, though, if we use it in a flexible way to gain insight into what happens with denial. If we paraphrase her stages, it might look something like this:

1. *Denial*—"No, not me." This is a typical reaction when a person is told that he or she is alcoholic.

2. *Rage and anger*—"Why me?" The alcoholic resents the fact that others can continue to drink. God is a special target for anger, since He is regarded as arbitrarily imposing this "curse" on them.

3. *Bargaining*—"Yes, me but . . ." The alcoholic admits the fact of "problem drinking" but tries to strike bargains. "I'll only drink wine." "I'll only drink on the weekends." "I'll go to church more." "I'll see a psychiatrist." "I'll cut down." He or she promises to be good, but as Dr. Kubler-Ross notes with the dying, "What they promise is totally irrelevant, because they don't keep their promises anyway."

4. *Depression*—"Yes, me." The alcoholic enters a state of depression, getting ready for letting go.

5. *Acceptance*—"I'm an alcoholic, and now what can I do about it?" We're talking about accepting the fact that the disease exists, and that this is the first step to recovery. It's an assertion of life rather than of death.

One of the ways people deny their alcoholism is to attempt to drink moderately or socially after they have not had a drink for some time. This, quite simply, doesn't work. Their efforts to go back to social drinking may be a denial of the fact that they were ever an alcoholic in the first place, or it may be a denial of the fact that they *still* have the disease. Once you have the disease, you always have it. No amount of wishing will change that. The failure rate for people who try to go back to moderate drinking is astounding.

An article in the *San Francisco Chronicle** cites a study done at Patton State Hospital near San Bernardino. Ten years ago, a select group of twenty men left the hospital with special cards identifying them as alcoholics who had been retrained as "social drinkers."

A study of these men over the past decade reveals, according to the report, that "most subjects trained to do controlled drinking failed from the outset to drink safely. The majority were rehospitalized for alcoholism treatment within a year after their discharge from the research project."

Overall, the report states that only one man was able to go back to social drinking, and he had been misclassified in the first place and was not really an alcoholic. Of the remaining nineteen, the report showed:

Four are dead of alcohol-related causes. For example, one was found floating face down in a lake, and a sec-

*"Alcoholic Retraining 'Failure,' " *SF Chronicle,* June 28, 1982.

ond committed suicide by jumping off a pier. Both had blood-alcohol levels three times that considered to be legally drunk.

Eight continued to drink excessively despite repeated damaging consequences such as job loss, arrest, marital breakup, or hospitalization for alcoholism and related serious illnesses.

Six have now abandoned their efforts to do controlled drinking and have become abstinent.

One is missing, but was certified as "gravely disabled" because of drinking, about a year after being discharged from the project.

Remember, these people were "retrained" to drink socially! Getting through the denial is the first step to recovering from the disease. To the extent that we, as individuals and as a society, can let go of our attitudes about alcoholics and alcoholism it's going to be easier for alcoholics to do the same thing.

WHY ALCOHOLISM LOOKS LIKE A PSYCHIATRIC DISEASE

It's not surprising that people often operate under the delusion that alcoholism is a psychiatric illness. The psychological effects of the physical disease often make it look that way.

Alcohol is a strong drug. It is a sedative hypnotic that causes irritation of the central nervous system. For a person who is already sensitive to the drug, alcohol can make them behave abnormally.

Since this is true not only when they are under the influence of the drug, but also when they are in withdrawal, it's happening a good percentage of the time if the disease has advanced to the middle or late stages. Irrationality, unpredictability, blackouts, irritability, broken promises, irresponsibility, inappropriate sentimentality—all these things make the alcoholic look like a mental case. The fact is that once the alcoholic is free of the physical effects of the drug (which can take from six months to two years), he will be no more or less mentally disturbed than the rest of the population—whatever that means!

"DRUGGISM" OR "SEDATIVISM"

I think it's a mistake to make alcoholism such a special disease, whether we look on it with horror or whether we see it as something that is so different and spectacular that we are unique individuals for having it. It's none of those things. It's just another disease, like heart disease or diabetes. And it's just another addiction, like addiction to caffeine, to chocolate or to being a victim. Recovery will be so much easier once people can see alcoholism for what it really is.

"NONADDICTING" SUBSTANCES

A substance doesn't have to be heroin to get somebody hooked. It can be as innocent a substance as gumdrops. It's the substance, coupled with the person, that sets up the addictive cycle.

Feelings produce (and often can be produced by) various physiological and chemical changes. The next time you are angry or sad, stop for a minute and feel what is going on with your body. It will feel different from the way it feels when you aren't angry or sad.

The natural impetus of the body is to feel good. When you take away a substance that, for whatever reasons, makes it feel good, then you produce discomfort that is both physical and psychological in nature. Even though the addiction appears to be psychological, withdrawing the substance produces physical changes that must be dealt with.

That's why people can get addicted to substances the FDA thinks are just fine—like chocolate, potato chips, bread, peanuts, jujubees, or whatever. The substances *are* just fine. It's the combination of the substance, the person, and his or her reaction that produces the addiction.

ADDICTION IS LIFE MULTIPLIED BY 100.

By now, perhaps you have noticed that human beings are prone to addictions and that life can be full of them. One becomes addicted to that which one has determined to be necessary for survival. Patterns of addiction can be translated into any area of life. It's all a matter of degree. Some people feel that they cannot survive without screaming (they call it "expressing their feelings"). Others feel they must withdraw (they call it self-control), others must eat jelly beans (otherwise they couldn't run the country), and others must drink alcohol (or they couldn't ask a girl to dance).

By observing the psychological and physical nature of addiction, we can learn much about the nature of the Robot and its need to attach itself to something for survival. We can also experience the power of the Observer and begin to learn how to run our addictions rather than have them run us.

EIGHT

If Your Child's an Alcoholic or an Addict

WHERE IS THE PROBLEM—WITH YOUR CHILD OR WITH YOU?

The first step in determining whether your child is an alcoholic or an addict is to calm down. Even if he is, you aren't the first parent who has been through this and lived. Remember that many of the symptoms of alcoholism are also symptoms of rebellion, so take a deep breath before you do anything else.

Second, observe your child's symptoms clearly. Is he an addict or not? You've read the early symptoms of alcoholism in the last chapter. The following are some other symptoms likely to manifest themselves in teenagers. To determine if your child is manifesting them, you need to be able to observe rather than react.

Is there alcoholism or addiction in the family?
drunk driving charges
bad or deteriorating grades
red eyes
getting drunk frequently
sleepiness

anything missing around the house
(silver, jewelry, money, etc.)
heavier than usual rebellion
resentment
withdrawing
temper
irritability
flu
headaches
intolerance
blackouts
booze or other drugs in the room or car
other behavioral changes
a general malaise
tension, lack of communication
defensiveness

Obviously, every time your kid has a headache or the flu you
don't have to be concerned that he might be an alcoholic. These,
along with the symptoms listed in the previous chapter, are just
some of the things to look for. Even if your child has a great
many of them, it doesn't necessarily mean he's an alcoholic.

IT COULD BE A BAD CASE
OF REACTION

There are two possibilities:

Your child is not an addict. He may have a bad case of rebellion, or a strong reaction to his suspicion that *you think* he's
an addict, but it's not the substance he's addicted to, it's the
rebellion.

Your child is an addict. If this is the case, he's probably
feeling defensive and scared. He's probably not going to respond very well to someone who approaches him in a panic.

IF YOUR CHILD IS REBELLING,
OR IF YOU'RE NOT SURE

Before you set out to "prove" whether he is an addict or having a problem with alcohol or other drugs, look at your own positions. Are you imposing your attitudes on him and treating them as the Truth? If you're getting resistance from him, you can be pretty sure that you have some fixed position(s) or attitude(s) that have become fairly rigid. Resistance requires something solid to oppose, or it dissipates.

If rebellion is the problem, he may be exaggerating his "alcoholic symptoms" in order to get even more of a rise out of you. If he can get you convinced that he's an addict, and then turn out *not* to be, you will look ridiculous. He will be right, right, right, and you will be dead wrong.

Underneath that, of course, he may be very hurt or angry that you would "think that badly of him." Remember, kids have their own filters and attitudes about alcoholism and they are almost always negative. If you don't trust him any more than that, he'll show you.

He may just be using alcohol or other drugs to rebel against your attitudes in general. You don't like booze, so he does. It becomes his favorite thing. Or you criticize her friends, and this is a great way to get back at you. When she smokes grass, it makes you feel powerless, just the way she feels when you criticize her friends.

Or you drink, so he smokes dope or drops acid. The truth is, he doesn't like you to drink because he sees how you act when you do. He's going to show you not only that a) he's just as grown up and tough as you are, because he uses substances, too, but also that b) his substances are better than yours. His give him insight and make him enlightened; yours make you sloppy and irrational. Not only that, but his using them makes you furious—more so than anything else he could do. He's got all the cards when he uses those drugs.

Or you overeat, so he overdrinks. He's going to show you just what it feels like to be on the other side, watching someone do something that's harmful to themselves. And you don't dare criticize him, because you're as bad or worse about your food as he is about his booze. In fact, he's almost hoping you *do* criticize him, so he can lay into you about the food. You know it, so you lie low.

If you don't know whether your child is an addict or not and you want to start unraveling the interlocking attitudes and reactions between you and your child, there are several things you can do.

Continue to work on your communication skills.

Whether or not he is an addict, you won't get anywhere with him if you can't communicate with him. At this stage you want to open up general communication. This is not the time to confront the drug problem head-on—not until you have sought help for yourself. Read the paper. Talk to him about the local sports teams. He may laugh at your lack of knowledge. That's great! He's beginning to interact. Get *him* to educate you! Invite his friends in, even if you don't care for them. You might as well get acquainted and then you can at least ask how they are. Don't expect miracles. All you may get from him are grunts and groans. That's okay. At this point, that's communication. Take him fishing or to a ball game. Don't worry whether he talks. Just do it.

Many teens can't stand the thought of being with their parents, but I've found that recreating some of the things we did when they were small will bring back memories to talk about. "Remember the time Dad went onto the ice with his skate guards on and slid all over the place?" "Remember how Mom screamed when we found ourselves in a graveyeard on that camping trip?" Forcing the issue *occasionally* won't hurt them or you. Kidnap them if necessary; once you get them out of the house, you just might have fun.

Listen to their records. It won't deafen you, it just seems like it will. Ask them questions. Be willing to be stupid and outdated. Let them laugh at you. My kids think I'm "weird." They also think I'm kind of cute—and we do communicate!

This is the best investment of time and energy you could make, and it will probably provide you with the key to finding out what he's drinking. If you're honest with yourself and with him, then sooner or later he's going to be honest with you.

Find a qualified group or therapist.

This is for you, not him. He's probably not interested in this, and it could produce a negative reaction if you suggest it. You need all the support you can get, and there's no shame in asking for it. It's not an admission that there's anything wrong with either you or with your child. It's an honest statement that, "I want to do the best job I can in this situation, so I'm going to use all the resources available to me."

Attend Alanon. Join Parents Who Care. Find a qualified therapist who understands addiction and its affects on *you*.

If none of this is available in your community, start something yourself. If you have a community of over 100 people, you've got enough people with addiction problems in their families to start an Alanon group. Get information on how to do so from the Alanon headquarters in New York City.

Get clear information from your child on what his symptoms are.

Are those red eyes from drinking, smoking pot, or staying up late? Or from an eye infection? What's going on here? It's okay to ask. If you're truly interested in his well-being, and not just indignant that he might be doing something of which you don't approve, that will communicate itself to him.

Are her grades getting worse because she's boozing it up, or because she doesn't like her teachers, or because this year she's more interested in boys than in studying? Again, you're simply looking for the truth from the point of view of supporting her, not criticizing her. Begin asking questions—without accusation. "I know lots of kids smoke pot. Are the effects anything like booze?" "Is that what makes people's eyes red?" "Have you ever mixed drugs?" "What happens when people combine pot and cocaine?"

She may say she doesn't know, she's never touched the stuff. Then ask if her friends do, and what are their reactions. Try to put her in the position of "expert." If you're getting no response, stay in the hands of your group or therapist. They will give you guidance.

Be willing to stand up for your standards
without trying to prove that you're "right".

Any time you try to be right with your kids, particularly with your teenage kids, you're asking for trouble. That doesn't mean, however, that you have to abdicate your responsibility as a parent and not stand up for your standards.

As we pointed out earlier, if it's not okay for your kids to drink and drive, tell them so in no uncertain terms.

Listen to their reactions, hear what they say, and stick to what you believe in. Describe clearly the consequences of a broken rule, and follow through.

IF YOUR CHILD IS AN ADDICT

The first step is the hardest, because it goes against a lot of the attitudes you have about being a parent. *The first step is to get help for yourself.* You're not going to be any good to him or to yourself if you go into this situation half-crazed without any kind of support for yourself.

Some places you might look for assistance and support are Alanon, the National Council on Alcoholism, or a qualified counselor. (Many counselors who claim to be qualified in this field are not. It's best to check with your local affiliate of the National Council on Alcoholism.) Tell them your situation and ask where you can go for help. These organizations will not tell you how to manipulate your child into therapy. They are there to assist you with your feelings and reactions.

Stop for a minute. Look at your own feelings. They probably include fear, anger, guilt, frustration, and hopelessness. You need help not only to support you emotionally, but because the chances are excellent that you are or have been functioning as an enabler co-alcoholic without knowing it.

The next step is to get more training in the kinds of communication skills we've talked about in this book, or to simply start practicing what we've discussed. No one can hear this information, or read this book, and expect to go out into the world and communicate perfectly with everyone 100 percent of the time. It takes practice, patience, and attention, but it's worth it.

Reread this book. And reread it again. The principles laid down here will work. But they must be absorbed, not learned in the sense of memorized. They must become part of you. There are counselors trained in Intervention—an effective communication system developed by Vernon Johnson which gives alcoholics the feedback they need to begin seeking recovery. Buy Johnson's book *I'll Quit Tomorrow* (see Bibliography), and use the principles he describes.

Don't wait until you think you're "good enough." You get good at communication by communicating. Start now!

IF YOUR CHILD WON'T RESPOND

There are some situations in which, no matter what you do, your child just won't respond to you. It may be that, no matter how beautifully you respond or how well you communicate, you just aren't the person with whom he needs to handle what is going on with him. There's no shame in that; it's just the way it is. It doesn't mean you've done anything wrong or that there's anything you could have done to handle the situation better. If that's the case, don't be afraid to use all the resources available to you.

You may even have to be willing to turn your child over to the care of someone else, whether it's an individual or an institution. That may look like a failure to you, but it's not. You're doing something to solve the problem, rather than perpetuating it by trying to handle it yourself when that is clearly not going to work. Trying to keep your "dirty laundry" at home is rarely the solution. Again, you have to go back to the question of what your purpose is with your child. If it's to support him, then you'll need to do whatever supports him, whether it makes you look good or not.

All you're doing by letting someone else take over is simply acknowledging the truth which is that, for whatever reason, you have no power in the particular situation—and you want your child to be with someone who can help him. That, of course, will require a bit of letting go. Remember that letting go of your child doesn't mean that you are abandoning him. It just means that you're willing for him to have his process and for you to have yours. You're not giving him license to go out and do anything he wants; you're putting him in the care of someone who can enforce standards and allow him to free himself.

PART III

FAMILY DYNAMICS AND ALCOHOL

NINE

Homeostasis, or the Benefits of Losing One's Balance

WHAT IS HOMEOSTASIS?

Homeostasis, according to the Random House dictionary, means "the tendency of a system to maintain internal stability owing to the coordinated response of its parts to any disruptive situation or stimulus attempting to disturb its normal condition or function."

More simply, homeostasis is the process by which something finds internal stability and balance. If anything gets out of whack, homeostasis brings it back into line. The word comes from "homeo" (the same) and "stasis" (standing), and means standing or staying the same. Everything in nature seeks balance, and operates within the principle of homeostasis: cells, plants, human bodies, human minds—and families.

In families, homeostasis means that there is a certain way things are set up, that everyone has a specific role to play in the balance. Each family member can make predictable reactions to any given situation based on what their role is within the family. One of the purposes of homeostasis in families, you see, is to avoid the unknown.

HOW IT WORKS

Here is how homeostasis might look in a diagram:

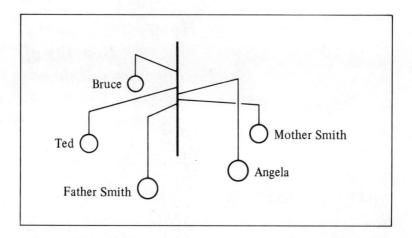

It looks a little like a mobile, a perfectly balanced piece of art. Everybody has their place, and the equilibrium is maintained. There is a difference between mobiles and homeostasis in families, however. Mobiles are stable because they are flexible. In order to be truly stable, a thing has to be somewhat flexible. Homeostasis in many families is anything but flexible.

We often base our selfhood, our sense of who we are, on our role in the family homeostasis, and we'll go to any lengths to protect it. If the alcoholic gets sober, if the troublemaker joins the seminary, if there's an illness somewhere—then everybody's going to try to restore the old balance, or, failing that, to find new positions to retain their sense of identity. After all, it's better to be a black sheep than a lost sheep.

I should mention here that other groups—office groups, bridge clubs, friendship groups—tend toward a family-like homeostasis. How often have you heard someone at the office say, "I can't believe it! Every time I'm around Lucy, I feel like I'm with my mother!" We may run away from it in our families, but whether we're aware of it or not, mom, dad, and our siblings are around every day in some form or another.

THE ADVANTAGES OF HOMEOSTASIS

Some predictability is desirable. Homeostasis keeps the family from chaos. The security afforded by homeostasis, however, can be a dubious advantage. Because everyone knows how to react and how to relate, they're always right about everything. Also, no matter how terrible the family looks or how dreadful their particular brand of equilibrium is, anything is better than the unknown—and there's always somebody to blame.

Usually one person in a family takes the role of troublemaker. He acts out for the rest of the family, and is blamed every time something goes wrong. You might think that the guy who's always acting out and getting all the blame would want to break the mold, but that's not necessarily true. If he suddenly turned into a great, easygoing person with no problems, his identity would be lost. The advantage to him is that he gets a lot of attention and unlimited excuses for his problems.

THE DISADVANTAGES OF HOMEOSTASIS

Obviously, a rigid homeostasis will stunt growth and freedom for the people involved. When one person tries to change, the family often acts to get him back into line.

In addition to preventing growth and freedom, a frozen homeostasis strips people of responsibility for their lives. Things are the way they are, rather than the way people would like them to be "because of the situation, and there's nothing we can do about it."

This is particularly true in alcoholic families. Everything would be fine if it weren't for the alcoholic, or, everything would be fine if this child weren't such a troublemaker. But as the situation is now, "there's just nothing we can do about it." They couldn't make it work even if they tried, so why bother? And besides, it's not their fault or their responsibility.

In a rigid homeostasis, there is no strength; the family loses its power as a unit. The energy becomes dispersed, disunified, and focused on issues that bring no satisfaction. The intrinsic power of the family is, if not destroyed, at least diminished—to be replaced by the false sense of unity created by the homeostatic crisis.

The point of maintaining homeostasis is to keep the family protected so that nothing can go wrong. Actually, however, things stay the same for a while and then they get worse.

For things to get "better," someone has to grow. Better means happier, more fun, freer. Those things just aren't going to happen if no one's allowed to move.

Let's look at a specific example.

THE SMITHS

Father Smith is an alcoholic and, in one way or another, everybody else's life revolves around him. He's a brilliant engineer, and has risen through the ranks to become vice-president of his company. No one at work or at the country club knows Father Smith is an alcoholic; they think he's just a jolly social drinker. His family, however, knows he's out of control.

One reason so few people know Father Smith is an alcoholic is that Mother Smith covers his tracks everywhere, making excuses for him at the country club, at work, and with their friends. She's a "good Christian woman" whose whole life has become centered around Father Smith; she makes sure that her children understand the evils of alcohol and finds more and more subtle ways to let her friends know what a saint she is.

Their daughter Angela, seventeen, is the troublemaker in the family. She's angry with her father for being something as disgraceful as an alcoholic, for being nasty when he's drunk, and for generally ruining all of their lives. She's angry at her mother for putting up with him, and she's angry at the world. She may not graduate, largely because she's become the drug queen of her high school. She smokes grass on a daily basis, drops acid or PCP at least once a week, and the substances to be found in her room could compete with any pharmacy in the city. She's surly and contemptuous, and knows there's only one cause for her (and everyone else's) trouble: Father Smith. She makes sure he finds out she's sleeping with both the tight end on the football team and with the bass player in the school's punk rock band.

Son Bruce, fifteen, is just the opposite. He's sweet and soft-spoken, always holding Mother Smith's hand and going to church with her—a real "turn-the-other-cheeker." He cleans up after Father Smith, even when Father Smith tries to beat him up, and makes sure he doesn't hurt Mother Smith. (He doesn't have to worry about Angela. Her tight end has shown her some of his judo tricks and she's just itching for Father Smith to come at her.) Bruce doesn't drink at all, much to his mother's relief. He gets straight A's and holds down a twenty-hour-a-week job at McDonald's. Bruce is so perfect he almost puts Mother Smith to shame.

Ted, thirteen, is the victim of it all. What can you expect of him with a father who's a drunk, a mother who's a religious fanatic, a sister who's a junky, and an older brother who's giving the Christ child competition? Ted has been labeled emotionally disturbed. He doesn't talk, except under duress, and seems not to be able to look anybody in the eye. He and his psychiatrist have finally come up with the cause of all his problems. When Ted was only four, Father Smith came home drunk and hit him so hard he fell down. After that, it was all downhill.

So everybody in the Smith family has his place, and they all know where they stand with one another and especially with Father Smith. Then Father Smith stops drinking.

All of a sudden, Mother Smith has nothing to do with her life. She has no sense of herself, no means of self-validation, and no place to put all that energy. She is hospitalized with a nervous breakdown. Angela is now truly a rebel without a cause. She has nothing against which to direct her anger. In desperation, she mixes alcohol with so many other drugs she can't even remember what they were, and runs the family station wagon up a tree. She's in a wheelchair now, and takes over Ted's place as the family victim.

Bruce has no one to be good *to, about,* or *for.* What's more, nobody pays any attention to him anymore. Now it's Father Smith who's the saint. Bruce figures there's no percentage in this sainthood game, and does an about-face. Within a few months, he's freebasing so much cocaine he has to push it to support his habit. He's now in the troublemaker slot Angela used to occupy.

And Ted? Now that Father Smith looks so great to everyone, no one believes that he's disturbed because of Father Smith, so he gives it up. In fact, it looks to Ted as though the only way he can keep up this adversary relationship with Father Smith is to beat him at his own game. Ted, therefore, turns into the family saint. He slides right into the slot Bruce used to occupy.

Now there's a new homeostasis, but it looks a lot like the old one. No one is really much happier, but things are once again predictable. There was a lot of movement, but nobody really went anywhere.

HOMEOSTASIS IN THE FAMILY
WITH ALCOHOLISM

From observing the Smiths, you can see that to some extent the focus of everybody's life has been what to do with or about the alcoholic. When the alcoholic starts getting sober, there may be a subtle, even unconscious temptation to want things back the way they were, to regain the familiar ground, even if it means the alcoholic has to keep drinking.

Being sober is as new, unknown, and unfamiliar to him as it is to his family. He will tend to gravitate back toward the familiar, especially if he's getting conscious or unconscious pressure from his family to do so.

In one family in which the father was an alcoholic, the daughter weighed 200 pounds. She got terrible grades and was drinking excessively. One day the father quit drinking, began paying bills, set a curfew for his daughter, and began discussing her homework with her as he hadn't done in years. The daughter was miserable because she no longer had an excuse for all her failures. She wanted more than anything for the situation to get back to normal. She began to drink in front of her father and finally started spiking his coffee to get him drunk!

SHIFTING HOMEOSTASIS:
LOSING ONE'S BALANCE

If only one person has the courage to shift his or her position consciously, without caring what anybody thinks, then everybody else will have to shift, too. They may scramble for a while, but if that one person stays in response to the situation rather than moving back into reaction, then he or she can begin to break up the pattern.

In order to make that move, the person has to be willing to let go of his attitudes and points of view about how the other family members are or should be. He must be willing for everybody else to be upset with him, or to ignore him in the hope that he'll just sink back into place.

The shift doesn't have to involve alcohol or other drugs. It could be that you decide to stop smoking, or overeating, or talking about people behind their backs, or making the other people in the family wrong. All anyone has to do is alter a customary pattern of behavior to toss the whole family homeostasis up in the air. And it only takes one person to do it.

WHAT TO EXPECT WHEN
THE SHIFT STARTS

You might have a picture of how things are going to be once the pattern is smashed, and think that now everybody is going to be perfect and relate to one another lovingly and openly as model human beings. That's not likely.

In fact, things may get a lot worse before they get better. If the alcoholic is your teenaged daughter, you may be criticized for not caring more—now that you no longer cry and look depressed all the time. You may be accused of being too lenient for not grounding her every weekend. The other children may be upset because you no longer treat them like the "good ones." They'll accuse you of trying to mess up the happiness of the family. They'll suggest that you've flipped out and you should see a psychiatrist. They'll want to make *you* the one to blame. They'll tell you you're just on a new kick and that it'll wear off in a week.

That's the worst that could happen. It may not be that bad. They might even hear what you say and think it's a great idea. Don't count on it, though. That kind of thing usually comes later.

It will come, sooner or later, if you're willing to stick to your guns and keep responding. Ultimately, it's going to get to them. You'll probably be a lot more pleasant to be around, happier with yourself, and more supportive of them. That's a very hard combination to beat.

STAYING IN COMMUNICATION WITH YOURSELF

If you stay in communication with yourself during the time you're making the shift in the homeostasis, you could be in for some big surprises. At the very least, you're going to learn a lot about yourself.

Watch yourself as things start to shift. Have you started to get self-righteous about being the one to make the shift? What effect does that have on the other people in the family? Are you keeping focused on your purpose in doing it, rather than just being delighted to stir things up? Do you react or respond when people react to you?

If it's someone else rather than you who has shifted his position, what is your reaction? Are you as pleased as you thought you'd be that they made the change (from booze, cigarettes, food, or whatever)? Or are you a little threatened, frustrated, or disappointed?

Whether you are the person making the shift, or whether it is someone else in the family, be prepared to feel insecure, unloved, unneeded, and other uncomfortable emotions, because sometimes the process of growth is uncomfortable. However, you may feel none of those things. You may feel nothing but great, but it's best to be prepared.

DEALING WITH THE UNKNOWN

Whether you are the shifter or the shiftee, you will be facing the unknown. Whenever we undertake the unknown, we face three things: fear, resistance, and responsibility.

We're all afraid of what we don't know, and there's nothing to do but tell the truth about it. Everything and everyone is going to be *off*-balance for a while. Under those circumstances, responsiveness is essential.

There is no "bad guy," no one is right and no one is wrong. Everybody plays a part in the homeostasis. The point is rather, who's going to recognize their part and call a halt to it? Who's going to stop the merry-go-round? Who's going to break that dynamic of multiple and interlocking triggers and attitudes that goes on in homeostasis? It's certainly not going to be the person who's waiting for the other people to do it.

TEN

Bad Guys and Victims

SOCIETY'S ATTITUDE
ABOUT PARENTS: GUILTY!

Our society has the point of view that whatever happens to kids is their parents' fault. If they turn out to be a mess, the parents are to blame. If they turn out well, the parents can take the credit.

On the cover of *People* magazine for June 14, 1982, there is a picture of John Hinckley with the caption: "The Hinckley Case, Lessons for Every Parent." Though not always conscious, the immediate response of most parents when they see such a caption is fear. A headline like that is bound to jolt us. We know that, some way or another, our kid could get into trouble and *we* could wind up on the cover of *People* magazine. Even if it were just the local paper, it would be bad enough.

Sad to say, people tend to believe John Hinckley's father when he says, "I am the cause of John's tragedy. We forced him out at a time when he just couldn't cope." But some therapists and other professionals say that the only thing to do with someone exhibiting the kind of behavior John was, especially at his age (twenty-seven), is to move him out of the house. Other

experts will say that's the worst thing you could do. Still others
will say that he should have been moved to some kind of half-
way house. The point is that there are lots of different opinions
about what *should* have been done in the case of John Hinckley.
After all, hindsight vision is always 20/20. But one thing is certain: Mr. Hinckley is not the "cause" of John's tragedy. He did
everything he knew how to do at the time. John Hinckley pulled
the trigger. He "caused" the assassination attempt. The point
is, John's father, mother, teacher, psychiatrists, our society—
none are "to blame." Even John isn't "to blame." Yet at the
same time, all of them, including you and me, are responsible.

SOCIETY'S ATTITUDE ABOUT
CHILDREN: VICTIMS!

According to prevailing attitudes, no one has to be responsible
for anything because we *all* have someone else to blame. We
deny our children their ability to respond by giving them something or someone to blame. It's the school, the media, peer
pressure, their siblings, or their psychiatrists; anyone other than
themselves. There's always a scapegoat, and much too frequently, it's their parents.

It's like the song from *West Side Story,* "Gee, Officer
Krupke" in which the gang members blame their parents and
society for the fact that they became punks.

Interestingly enough, it's the parents who perpetuate this point
of view, for two reasons: a) If parents aren't to blame for the
bad things, then they can't take credit if the kid turns out to be
a success. Most parents aren't willing to give up the credit, so
they're not in a position to give up the blame; and b) Many parents are the victims of *their* parents. To relinquish this viewpoint, they would have to stop blaming their own parents for
any lack of success or emotional problems they might experience.

Researchers spend millions examining the issue of what kind of parent produces what kind of child. What do parents do that causes children to turn out in a particular way? What is seldom taken into account or too frequently rationalized away is that parents can raise two children in exactly the same way and they will turn out entirely differently. One will be aggressive and outspoken, and the other will be quiet and timid. One will be successful, and the other not so successful. One will be loving and the other not so loving. There are dozens of explanations for this—placement in the family, for example—but most don't hold much water.

It is possible that research to date has been looking in the wrong places. A better question may be: What kind of child produces what kind of parent? In fact, this kind of research is finally beginning to take place.

Let's look at a third possibility, however. What if we just stopped trying to fix blame? Once we stop fixing the blame we can begin to respond to the situation and correct it.

NOBODY LIKES TO FEEL GUILTY.

People will do almost anything to get away from the feeling of guilt. One thing they will do is *avoid it*. They try to do everything perfectly so that they can't ever be blamed for anything. If they don't manage to do everything just "right," then they have a myriad of good rationalizations, reasons, justifications, and excuses ready and waiting—anything to keep them from feeling guilty. This is the "perfect parent" syndrome.

Another thing people do with guilt is to *ignore it*. They will do anything they can to get rid of the feeling: take a drug, drink, eat, watch TV, become a workaholic, or get rid of the person who's making them feel guilty.

A third way of dealing with guilt is to *deny it*. These people pretend it doesn't exist, and refuse to feel anything at all. They come up with this one all the time: "Why should I feel guilty? I didn't do anything and I'm not about to have a guilt complex about it."

Bob's daughter Susan gets caught selling dope at school. Bob hates feeling guilty, so what does he do? He might *avoid it,* insisting that he and his wife had done everything right, had never even kept dope or prescription drugs in the house, so there's no way it could be their fault. He might *ignore it,* simply refuse to look at the issue and pour himself a couple of stiff drinks and go sit in front of the tube. Or he might *deny it* by insisting "Susan is just a normal kid doing what all kids her age do," or he might announce, "Well, that's not my problem. She fell in with the wrong crowd at school."

As parents, we will do anything to get rid of those guilty feelings, and there's always a way. The problem here, as elsewhere, is the business of resistance and persistence. When we try to get away from the guilt, to resist it, we only compound it and make it worse. We'll never get rid of it as long as we resist it. It will niggle away at us relentlessly.

One of the sneakiest methods people use to avoid feeling guilty (a real paradox) is to beat their breasts and say how guilty they are all the time. These people constantly apologize for everything they do, constantly tell you they are sorry, and generally make it known to the world that they are terrible people.

It looks as though they feel extremely guilty, but the truth is that they have such an act going that they have no real experience of being guilty. (They want pity for their "guilt.") There's nothing better than beating your potential critics to the punch, and assuming all the guilt before somebody else hands it to you.

THE GUILT/VICTIM CYCLE

If I think you are guilty of something, I will blame and punish you. If I think *I* am guilty, paradoxical as it may seem, then I will also blame and punish you. When I punish someone, they become my victim. Then I feel guilty, and I also feel victimized by them. Somehow, someone else is always to blame for my guilt. It's a vicious cycle. Guilt creates victims, and victims create guilt.

Here's how it works with the parent who abuses his child. Let's say that I'm your parent and I beat you. Now I'm a child beater, so I feel guilty. I have to find a reason why I hit you, so I can get rid of the guilt. It must have been your fault for screaming so loudly. Since you're to blame I punish you. Now I'm a child beater again, and feeling so guilty, that I feel victimized by you and have to beat you again to punish you. It goes on and on.

The punishment I deliver can be physical or psychological. The situation doesn't have to be as extreme as child beating. I can withdraw my love or act disapprovingly. I can do whatever's going to hurt you.

Suppose I've punished my daughter by grounding her for a week. I feel defensive about it, not recognizing that it's guilt. She withdraws from me (I call it being sullen) and I assume she thinks I'm being unreasonable. I then interpret everything she does along those lines. I say to myself, "Why is she looking at me like that? She must think I'm a nasty person." Now I've become her victim, so I want to strike out at her and make her feel guilty, too. And so it goes.

The sad thing is that through our guilt, we deprive our children (and incidentally, ourselves) of any accountability or responsibility. We set it up so that no one has to be responsible for anything.

MOVING FROM GUILT
TO RESPONSIBILITY

The Random House dictionary defines guilt as "that fact or state of having committed an offense, crime, violation, or wrong."

It defines responsibility as the state of being "answerable or accountable as for something within one's power, control, or management." Those two things—guilt and responsibility—are entirely different states. The two can't exist in the same space. If you're guilty, you can't be responsible. If you're responsible, you can't be guilty.

Guilt is a natural reaction when you've done something that violates your own code of ethics or that you're afraid is injurious to another person. If you don't feel guilty under those circumstances, (and those circumstances will arise as long as you're still a human being), then you may very well be in denial. The answer is to simply experience the guilt, and to use it as an indicator that you may have broken your own code, gone against your own standards, or not measured up to your own sense of what is right—and then respond to the situation, rather than react. The moment you use your guilt as a tool to correct a situation in a constructive, nonvindictive, nonblaming way, you are in response and the guilt will dissipate.

The reality of life is that almost every day we do something that's against our code. We talk about someone behind his back, or we cut somebody off in traffic, exceed the speed limit, make a snide remark, or have a nasty thought. Whether we want to admit it or not, most of us have judgments about those kinds of things. So we may feel guilty a lot of the time.

The fact is that most of us are being a little hard on ourselves. Maybe those codes are unrealistic and we can let go of some of them. For example, we think we should take the garbage out once a day, but we never do. Every time we look at it, we feel guilty. Maybe it's all right to take the garbage out every other day.

Another way to let go of guilt is to communicate. We may have a relationship or communication that needs responding to and we've postponed it so long we're feeling terribly guilty about it. Maybe we know Dad quit drinking and we've been meaning to write and tell him how terrific we think it is but with summer vacation and all we just haven't found time to do it. But it nags at us every day. Maybe it would be worth it to pick up to phone and say, "Dad, I'm sorry I haven't written or called, but I do want you to know how pleased I am that you're taking care of your health." Moving from guilt toward responsibility means taking some constructive action.

Some of us would like to get rid of our guilt by making the other guy do something. We want to make the alcoholic stop drinking, the child stop being a problem child, or the teachers stop doing whatever it is they're doing. That takes everything right out of our hands.

The first step is to take action ourselves. That might mean joining an organization like Alanon, AA, or a group of parents who are dealing with their children who have alcohol or drug problems. If we really do have terrible teachers in the school, then let's join the PTA and do something about it. By doing so, we begin to transform not only our own lives, but the lives of those around us.

That's what Candy Lightner did. The mother of a child who was killed in a drunk driving accident, Candy started MADD (Mothers Against Drunk Driving) to combat drunk driving. As a result of her efforts the drinking and driving laws in California have been transformed. Joining forces with parents in other states, she is responding, taking action.

Joining groups and taking actions, however, can also be used as an escape. If this is the case, our plan is apt to backfire.

Moving from guilt to responsibility means moving toward something, not away from it. It requires the willingness to rise, make a stand, take action, and it brings us the peace of at least knowing we've truly responded to something. It's important to remember that's all we can do. The outcome is not up to us.

TO BE A RESPONSIVE PARENT,
BECOME A RESPONSIVE CHILD

To become a responsive parent, *the key is to stop blaming or giving credit to your parents*. The majority of us are still reacting to our parents (or anyone who represents our parents), as we did when we were children, even if we're fifty years old. If we want things to get better, we've got to stop doing that. Blaming past generations isn't going to produce the kind of results we want. It just gives us an excuse for the mess we're in. Until we're willing to let go of blame, we can't possibly get out of the mess. To stop giving credit doesn't mean to stop giving respect, love, recognition, and thanks. It means taking responsibility totally for our own choices, successful or otherwise. So, for those of us who are still blaming our parents, in any way shape or form, the first question is: "Would I rather have a scapegoat or a better situation?" If the answer is a better situation, then we'll have to let go of blaming.

Remember, our parents could not have known all the things we know today. We have access to information about people, about families, about life, that wasn't available to them. They did the best they could with what they had, just as we're doing the best we can with what we have. If we stop blaming our parents for being in whatever state of evolution they they were in, then maybe our children can do the same with us.

We need to drop our victim role relative to our parents. Victims don't grow; they just turn into victimizers. As long as we feel victimized by our parents, we will believe *our* children are victims. We'll have to, to protect our own victim status. And our kids will begin to see themselves as victims. They will feel guilty and the cycle will start all over.

This is very important in the family with alcoholism. There is a tendency to view the alcoholic and/or his family as victims of society, and of their parents. If we hold that attitude, we reject the alternative that everyone involved is a capable individual, powerful enough to take responsibility for their own lives. In my seminars, I recently worked with three generations of one family. Grandmother was a newly recovering alcoholic. Mother, at age forty, was still blaming her for her own failed marriage. ("You didn't set a good example for me.") Mother had a teenage son who was showing symptoms of addiction to marijuana and that was the grandmother's fault, too, because she hadn't "nurtured" mother enough, so of course the mother hadn't nurtured her son. As you can see, mother and grandson had it all wrapped up. They didn't have to take the responsibility for anything.

HOW TO LET GO OF
BLAMING OUR PARENTS

The answer is simpler than you could possibly imagine. Just forgive them. There's no "how to." You either do it or you don't. I know that sounds glib. But the truth is, it's a very simple thing to do.

All you have to do is make a statement, a commitment that you want to forgive them. It doesn't mean the anger, the resentments, and the pain are gone forever. Sometimes there are more tears and sadness after you forgive them than before, especially at first. What you've done is actually confronted the issue, and brought it to the surface along with those unconscious feelings.

Forgiveness opens up experience. Quite often we begin to feel things that have been buried for a long time. Experiencing opens communication. It's all right to let our parents know our experience, as long as we're willing to hear theirs.

Sometimes people rush to their parents and say, "You did *this* to me and you did *that* to me!" That kind of communication doesn't convey anybody's experience or derive from responsibility. To tell somebody your experience is to say, "When you went out of the room and turned off the lights, I was frightened. I've been punishing you for that for years, and I'd like to stop." That will make it possible for them to tell you their experience. You might be surprised by what you hear.

And, don't think you need to deny yourself this experience if your parents have died. Write a letter, or communicate with their picture. The point is for *you* to take responsibility, forgive them, and communicate. Believe me, it works.

ELEVEN

Process

WHAT IS PROCESS?

Process is "an on-going development with many changes." Our process in life is our movement toward self-knowledge, toward the ability to experience and love all of ourselves, and open ourselves completely to other people. The growth that we've been talking about throughout this book is process. It is the most natural, necessary, and beneficial thing in the world, because it is our personal development. And no matter how old or how wise we get, it never ends.

We keep seeing new things about ourselves, and letting new things emerge out of the process. *But we never get a finished product*, because growth is always taking place.

I had a friend who at thirty was delighted because she'd finally handled her relationship with her mother. She had come to the point where she and her mother could be friends and communicate with one another. That had always been such a big issue for her that she figured if she had any more growing to do, it would be in minor ways and it would be a snap to handle after this.

Was she surprised to discover that once she had her relationship with her mother handled, there was still her father. And men in general. And money. And weight. And so on. It was like peeling off the layers of an onion. That was upsetting to her at first, but once she realized that it was only a process and that process is what human beings go through in life, she could relax and enjoy it. The game goes on forever; only the players and the equipment change.

Process, the way I see it, is the greatest show in town. It's one exciting discovery after another. Sometimes it's uncomfortable, but it's usually even more fascinating than it is painful. It's like being at the movies all the time, only it's a movie of your own life and it's free. Not only does process enrich your experience of yourself and others, it's great entertainment as well.

OUR CHILDREN'S PROCESSES

Children's lives are nothing but process. The same can be said for our lives, but it's more obvious with kids. If you look at the first three years of life, you see nothing but change and development. It's exciting, but as time goes on, that part of us that longs for certainty and a status quo to hang onto, sometimes wants them to stop changing, to be finished, to be complete. We want them to already have the good manners, the clean rooms, the good grades in school. But they keep changing, right before our eyes. We can hardly even keep track of it.

First they're sweet, then awful, then docile, then rebellious. And they always seem to get stuck in those "bad" places! We, of course, would like it if they just stayed in a "good" phase. But would we? Being stuck in something we happen to like is still being stuck. Unfortunately, sometimes when they get stuck in the "good" places we're so relieved we don't even notice that they're stuck.

This occurs frequently in families in which one or both of the parents are alcoholics. Sometimes a child in these families seems overly responsible. The kid gets terrific grades, is president of this or that club, *plus* putting up with the alcoholic(s).

One of my dance students was a good student, a terrific dancer, and involved in lots of school activities, although her mother was an alcoholic. Then one day she had a nervous breakdown. She just couldn't function anymore. There are enough of these cases for us to know that it's not healthy for a child to get trapped in the "good" places any more than it is for him to get stuck in stealing or drinking or taking other drugs. It's just the other side of the same coin, and neither one is healthy.

There will be times when we won't like how our child's process looks at all. When we notice that he's staying there, we need to look and see if our resistance might be contributing to the situation.

It's almost as frightening for us to watch our children enter the unknown as it is to enter it ourselves, perhaps even more so. Sometimes we resist their process not because we don't like where they are *now*, but because we don't like where they might be *next*.

I talk to parents all the time who say, "Well, I can't change anything because if I make a move, things will be worse. If I say they can't have the car, they'll steal one." The sad thing about that is that, without the opportunity to learn from the consequences of his actions, the child can't continue with his process.

COMPETING WITH OUR CHILDREN

Most parents wouldn't want to admit it, but a real process stopper is competition with our kids. This is subtle and usually not conscious. Sometimes we are jealous of their success and don't want to be outdone by them. It's very embarrassing to have our children invalidate us by doing something differently from the way we did it, and having it turn out better.

One sure way to minimize your children's success is to attempt to stop their process so that they can't go forward and get on to the next thing. For example, the mother of a daughter who's just beginning to look stunning when mother is starting to fade a bit might feed her kid chocolate to fatten her up a little and give her pimples. By the same token, children often try to stop their parents' process. The daughter who feels threatened by her mother's attractiveness might suggest she wear the latest styles, in an unconscious attempt to make her look ridiculous.

My mother still feels guilty about what happened between grandma and the grocer. My mother was a year old when my grandmother was widowed. There were five kids and they lived in a small town. The local grocer fell in love with my grandmother and wanted to marry her, but the kids would have nothing to do with it. They wanted mom doing the things that moms did, and they didn't want any competition or anybody interfering in their lives. They did everything they could to maintain the status quo. The situation became so unpleasant for my grandmother that she took the kids and moved out of town.

It can work either way. The kids can compete with parents and parents can compete with the kids. Parents sometimes get a little queasy about the thought that they might be competing with their kids. They think it's terrible and can't believe they might do something so perverted. Actually, it's not that unusual or abhorrent. We're all people, and sometimes people compete with one another. Being parents—or children—doesn't make us saints.

WHAT HAPPENS
WHEN PROCESS STOPS

When process stops, usually because we or someone close to us is resisting it, it's like a broken record. It gets stuck, and repeats itself over and over. There's no way to get over it until that particular groove or step in the process has been fully experienced, and the particular lesson learned.

The way to unstick a process, whether it's your own or someone else's, is to let whatever is happening at the moment just happen. At this point it's important to emphasize the difference between experiencing the process and acting it out. When I say "let it happen," what I mean is to let the feelings, thoughts, desires be experienced. So, if I feel like hitting my child, "letting it happen" means to *feel* it—not to do it! Allow whatever thought or feeling is there to just exist. Learn what you can from it, and let it go. Then you can move on to the next thought or feeling.

When their process is stopped, our kids can't grow or mature. If they happen to be in a "good" spot (in which they have a lot of opinions and thoughts that we agree with) we may give them so much approval that they stay there. The result is that they have the facade of maturity, but not the substance. They haven't learned to choose for themselves. They have decided on a particular stance in order to please somebody (us), in order to look good, or in order to be right, and there's nothing mature or responsive in that.

The clue that your children are stuck is when patterns start repeating themselves without being resolved. Your son might, for example, get arrested for drunk driving three times in six months, or he might study incessantly and never go out with his friends. In either case, something reactive is going on.

PROCESS FOR SURVIVAL
OR ALIVENESS

The basic direction of the process is determined by its context. If the context is survival, then the process will ultimately be a deadening process. The person will simply get better and better at surviving and avoiding the unknown. If the context or goal is aliveness, then the process will produce aliveness. They may look similar on the surface, but the clue is that processes for aliveness tend to move more quickly than processes for survival. There is more experimentation in them, and that means more change.

At any minute, we can switch a process from survival to aliveness. If Johnny is doing poorly in school, we can support him in holding his situation in either a context of survival or a context of aliveness. We can say, "Oh, no. This is terrible. This is the end of the world. If you don't make it here, it's all over." That's survival. Or we can recognize that Johnny just isn't a very good student, and we can support him in approaching the situation as a way to explore other parts of himself, and encourage him to participate in sports or music or whatever his interests are. We can ask for help from the school. We can tell him that if this really doesn't work for him, maybe we can find another school. Basically, we don't make him wrong for not being a good student, nor do we create a threatening environment for him. We support him in finding ways other than good grades for him to express himself.

It may seem more difficult to switch the process in what seems like an actual survival situation, for example, when your child is using alcohol. If Johnny, now in his teens, is experimenting with alcohol, it is essential to not make him wrong if you want to support him through this part of his process. By communicating openly with him about the effects of alcohol, his friends' reactions to it, and his opinions and feelings, you allow him to have a broader experience than he will have if it's a closed topic, or just a series of lectures from you.

MENTALLY EXPERIENCING A PROCESS

You can complete a process without actual experimentation. Research indicates that basketball players can improve their shots by practicing mentally. And from my seminar work I know that people can overcome fear of airplanes, resolve relationships with deceased parents, and mentally experience eating chocolate cake without ever having the actual experience occur.

Communication is a surefire way of helping them mentally experience things in a nondestructive way. Sharing one's thoughts, fears, and viewpoints often removes the need to act out on them.

PERMISSION VERSUS LICENSE

A distinction must be made between support or permission and license. Children need permission to have their process, but that doesn't mean we have to give them license to do anything they want.

Permission is formal or express allowance, or consent. To give permission is to afford opportunity or possibility. License is excessive or undue freedom, or liberty. Our children need permission, but not license.

As I said earlier, I think it's essential that, as parents, we set limits in the areas of life, death, and severe physical or emotional harm. But we can't set too many limits or our children won't have any room for their own processes.

If kids are not given room to have their process, they rebel— and in the big areas, not the little ones. In order to gain their selfhood, they have to do something big such as crash the car, come home drunk, or run away.

With a few clearly defined and consistently enforced rules, the child has an opportunity to experience life and to discover what does and doesn't work. That is very different from giving license to do anything he wants. When we give that kind of license, we're abdicating our responsibility to give him guidance.

The same principles of permission and license apply as much to you as they do to your child. You need permission to have your process, too. I'm always reminded of that mother in Ohio who went on strike. She refused to cook, clean, wash clothes, or do anything until the children began to take their share of the responsibility in the household. She was willing to have her process. She simply took a stance and stuck to it. And the great thing was that her kids came around. There's no guarantee that that's going to happen, of course, but we do know that our children will never have anything to come around *to* unless we take a stand. That means claiming our right as human beings to have our process.

LETTING GO OF YOUR CHILDREN'S PROCESS

Giving permission also means letting go. As I've said before, letting go doesn't mean abandonment, or giving up on somebody, or throwing someone overboard.

Sometimes I hear people say, "I've let go of the situation," or "I've let go of him or her." What they usually mean is that they've abandoned that person, thrown them out of the boat, cut them off, severed the connection between them so that they no longer have to deal with them. That's not letting go. When you let go of someone, they are still very much a part of your life, but you are no longer attached to their process. You care, but you're not reacting and machinating with them, stirring up trouble. You may even be closer to them than before. The difference is that you are willing to let them have their own process.

When you abandon someone, you usually don't let yourself feel anything toward them. When you've let someone go, there may be some very strong emotions involved. In fact, having let go, you may have taken the lid off some feelings that you haven't let yourself acknowledge in a very long time. You are still connected to the person. The person is still in your life, and once you take that rigid attachment away, all those feelings may come rising to the surface.

I had a friend who finally let go of her relationship with her twenty-year-old daughter who was addicted to amphetamines. She stopped trying to fix her and started just letting her lead her own life. When she let go, she felt for the first time all the sadness, fear, and guilt that had been there all along, but that she'd been stuffing down so she could hold on. She was then able to communicate those feelings to her daughter who, now that she no longer had a mother constantly nagging her and going through her purse looking for pills, decided to undergo treatment. For the first time a constructive move could be her own idea.

People are always asking, "But how do you let go?" There's no "how to." You just do it. Hold onto your right knee. Now decide to let go of your right knee. Now let go. That's all there is to it. Simply state repeatedly that you are letting go, and that you are committed to letting go. Hold to it as a choice you have made. Sometimes you will feel the release that comes with that choice. Other times, you will feel anger, sorrow, joy, depression, or elation. Those are all feelings that come along with letting go.

When you stop protecting your child from hurt, he just may get hurt. You're going to have to be willing to feel whatever that brings up for you. It's the price you pay for letting your child grow up according to his own lights, and that is the greatest gift you could give him.

The time we let go may be the first time we have actually allowed ourselves to experience our kids' pain, confusion, fear, joy, and failures, and it may be the first time we've really experienced our own. When we do this, we may need some kind of support. We are apt to be faced with a multitude of feelings—guilt, regret, fear, loss, confusion, anger, depression. For this reason we might want to go to a parents' group, Alanon, or find a good counselor. Sometimes a good friend can help in a situation like this. You have to be careful when you're using friends, though, because you can use them up awfully quickly.

It's a good idea to find a professional or group where you can get the kind of support you need.

It's best not to expect that kind of support to come from your spouse. Your spouse is going through his or her own process. Even if your relationship is stable, a child's addiction will put a strain on it. Worry, helplessness, guilt, anger, despair are apt to result in accusations and recriminations. Conscious or not, verbalized or not, these feelings will exist and each of you has enough to do in taking care of your own feelings. You don't need to dump them on each other. This doesn't mean don't communicate, but it does mean that the best thing would be for both of you, together or separately, to get some kind of personal support, and not to expect it from one another.

I know a couple whose daughter committed suicide. The parents were so angry at one another for not being able to support each other during the crisis that they got a divorce. Some other friends lost their son in a plane crash. In that case, they each found their individual support systems. If anything, their relationship became richer. As they each became stronger through their own support system, they began to support each other more and more.

COMMUNICATING BY EXAMPLE

We are part of humankind's process, too. We contribute to it by engaging our own processes, by growing, by taking risks, by responding, by venturing into the unknown, and by expanding our experience of life.

That's also how we set the example for our children. Lecturing to our children is a waste of time. The communication we really want them to get is our willingness to let go and allow the process to fulfill itself.

There's one example I always think of in relation to trusting the process. A young woman who was having a lot of trouble with alcohol and other drugs made repeated suicide attempts. Several times, she took too many pills and ended up in the bathtub with her wrists slashed. Every time she did that, her parents would jump into a very strong reaction.

One time, she cut her wrists but, as usual, she managed to have somebody find her. By now her mother, who was a nurse, was catching on. The father said, "We have to get her to the hospital—quick! We'd better hurry!"

The mother realized no arteries were severed and what she said was "I don't think there's any real hurry. I'm hungry, I'd like to stop and get a hamburger on the way to the hospital." Well, they did stop for a hamburger, and after that the relationship between that young woman and her parents changed.

A lot of people might say, "How cold and callous!" But the mother knew her daughter wasn't in a life-threatening situation. She didn't want to be manipulated by her daughter's threats anymore, and she trusted her own process. Her instinct was to put a stop to it, and she did. The daughter didn't make any more suicide attempts. She realized that the game was over and the jig was up. I know the outcome well, for I happen to be the daughter.

Process exists whether we like or not, and even whether we know it or not. All we do with our resistance is to slow it. Giving permission—not license—to ourselves and to our kids creates a context of letting go. If we can let go, we can allow our kids to teach us and we can teach them by example. The future will be happier and brighter for us individually, and as a species, if we can learn to evolve in that way.

TWELVE

Co-ism:
The Ultimate
Painkiller

CO-ISM

The word "co-alcoholic" was first coined by Jo Coudert, a woman who realized that alcoholism is a family disease and that family members are as much in need of support as the alcoholic. "Co's" can be parents, children, siblings, friends, bartenders, teachers, counselors—anyone whose life is hooked up with the alcoholic's process and whose relationship with him would change dramatically if the alcoholic's life changed.

If I'm the co-alcoholic and you're the alcoholic, I'm usually the one who looks like I have it all together. In fact, I look like a saint. I'm taking care of you, cleaning up after you, being responsible for all the things you mess up, and keeping the family together. My whole life is centered on you and your process. I'm here to save you, and to be the victim of your problem. All the time I'm thinking about you, rescuing you, saving you, being concerned with your welfare. The other thing I'm doing is avoiding any experience of my own life.

I don't have to be responsible for myself, because I have you to take care of. That's such a big job I can't be expected to do anything else. It's a great way to avoid looking at myself, and at the same time look like a saint and a martyr. People point to me and say, "What would he/she do if it weren't for Roberta?" I'm sure I'm doing it out of love, but it certainly is an odd way to love someone. Love has to do with letting someone go through their process and fulfill their potential. Consciously or unconsciously, the primary goal of the co-alcoholic is to keep the alcoholic stuck—all the while looking as though they are devoting their life to getting him unstuck. It becomes insidious.

A classic example of co-ism is the wife who protects her alcoholic husband, like Mother Smith in our earlier example. She makes sure they leave parties before he gets too drunk, calls his boss for him when he can't come in to work, gets a job herself to meet the financial responsibilities, defends him to the kids, and generally tries to cover his tracks. The result for him is that he has no experience of himself as an alcoholic or of what is happening to his life. He doesn't have to face any consequences, so he never realizes that he has the disease. She has taken care of everything for him. What she's really done is taken away his selfhood.

She's fine, though. There are a few friends who know, and they think she's terrific. Now that she's so busy, so consumed with having to keep him straight, she doesn't have to look at her own guilt about how her kids are turning out, or her concern that she's getting older and doesn't really think she's done much with her life. All of that is swept under the carpet, and she can console herself with the notion that it all would have turned out fine, if it hadn't been for her husband.

It's almost as if the co-alcoholic is addicted to the alcoholic in the same way that the alcoholic is addicted to booze. It's generally accepted that over 50 percent of marriages break up *after* the recovery of the alcoholic spouse. Why? Sometimes, because the co needs the alcoholic to continue drinking—for his own reasons.

Co-ism is also a disease of denial, just as alcoholism is. "Me, a co?! Not a chance! I want to help her!" But the truth is, the alcoholic has become the co's reason for being. All of the co's self-worth is tied up in a need to be needed. To remove the alcoholic from the co's center of attention would be to leave the co without a self!

It's hard to break out of the pattern of being a co, because sometimes the addiction to the alcoholic is reciprocal. If the co starts moving into his or her own sphere and getting interested in his or her own life and growth, the alcoholic feels threatened. If that's the case, it's easy for the alcoholic to create a crisis in the home and get the co right back into line. He may go on a binge, or threaten suicide—and usually the co will come running.

A more general example of co-ism is the way society treats alcoholism. Alcoholism is frequently ignored or condemned. Everybody throws up their hands. Nobody knows what to do, except to hope that those poor, weak-willed people will someday find themselves. There is no responsibility, either for the fact that alcoholism exists, or for the fact that society's attitude toward alcoholism actually contributes to it.

That may be the crux of the problem right there. What would our society find out about itself if it examined how it might be responsible for alcoholism? It's a lot easier to either ignore it or just say alcoholics are bad people.

IT DOESN'T HAVE
TO BE ALCOHOL

The co doesn't have to be hooked up to an alcoholic. It can be a drug addict; someone with a physical, mental or emotional disability; an aging parent—anyone with an apparent problem will do. The more hopeless the problem seems, however, the better.

Co-ism exists, to one degree or another, in most relationships. All that's necessary is an attachment to the other person's problem that's greater than your interest in your own growth—or his. This involvement becomes a way to avoid your own experience. It involves concern, protectiveness, alienation, and anger. And all of it is "because of the other person's problem."

More than anything, co-ism involves being attached. Remember, attachment simply means that my experience is dependent upon the other person's experience. What he does, says, thinks, and feels determines what I do, say, think, and feel. I'm always concerned whether he is happy or sad, in good shape or a mess, staying with me or leaving.

Attachment, of course, means I can't experience what the other person is experiencing. There's no room for that, because all the concern is on my own experience. I live in constant fear, because I have no control over my own experience and no idea what's going to happen next. I'm always trying to figure out what the other person's experience is or will be, so that I can react to it. Ironically, I'm actually completely oblivious to the other person's experience or well-being, which is a way of attempting to maintain the status quo.

Take, for example, the case of an overprotective father. He wants everything to be perfect for his child, and does everything but put him in a plastic bubble. The child can't go out for football, because he might get hurt. He can't have dinner at his friend's house, because who knows what kind of an environment that is? He can't stay out late, or go on weekend camping trips with the Scouts. The result is that the child either knuckles under and never learns anything, content to live the rest of his life in this bubble, or he rebels and turns out to be the town delinquent.

The point, however, is not what happens to the child. It's what happens to the co-ing adult. More and more of his life is consumed with concern and anxiety about what might happen to the boy. Soon, the parent has no life of his own. It's all focused on the child.

In extreme cases, the father's relationship with his wife might start to deteriorate; he'll start to leave his job undone at work; financial troubles will arise; and now somehow, it's all the boy's fault. None of this would have happened if he hadn't had to devote so much time, energy, and attention to the kid. He is a slave to a situation that he created.

All three of these cases of co-ism have something in common. All three—the father, the wife, and society—avoid looking at their own processes, and they all diminish the people for whom they co.

PHYSICAL REACTIONS

Co-ism is a state of mind coupled with physical reactions. The co's life is filled with crises and the periodic surges of adrenaline that accompany them. Dr. Paul Rosch, director of the American Institute of Stress, states that many people get "high" on their own adrenaline and can therefore become addicted to stressful situations. We've found that when the alcoholic stops drinking and everything gets calmed down, the co often starts getting lethargic or depressed. His body has literally become so used to the excess adrenaline that he needs it to feel "normal."

In working with alcoholics, we have to deal with the fact that their bodies have begun to need alcohol. It's not just their minds that want it; their bodies want it. In working with co's, we have to deal with the fact that their bodies want adrenaline. Their bodies demand adrenaline in order to function, just as the alcoholic's body demands alcohol.

CO-ISM REPEATS ITSELF

We've said that when the co loses his alcoholic, or whatever kind of person he was co-ing, he gets very depressed. He has nothing to live for, no sense of himself. He scans for someone else to co, and if no one immediately appears, he continues to feel depressed or useless until he finds someone. But one thing is certain: he will find someone. This may be why 50 percent of the children of alcoholics marry alcoholics, and why a person who has married one alcoholic and gotten divorced is quite likely to marry another—unless he or she realizes that co-ism is going on and breaks the pattern. If they don't, they can wind up being co's for the rest of their lives.

THE HEART OF CO-ISM

Remember the old refrain, "There's something wrong with me"? That's the part of ourselves that we'll do anything to avoid looking at.

The alcoholic and the co-alcoholic are almost always perfect reflections of each other's "something wrong." Here's how it works. Initially the co might feel that the fun-loving alcoholic balances the co's serious approach to life, but as the alcoholic's drinking progresses, the co discovers that the alcoholic is sloppy, irresponsible, out of control, and generally a mess—all the things the co most fears about herself. She's afraid that if she ever let go, all those things would come rushing to the surface and she'd be just as bad as the alcoholic. She'd manifest the very things she hates and fears most. To counteract that, she puts on the appearance of a meticulous, thoughtful, responsible, and in-control person.

The alcoholic, on the other hand, probably has a secret fear that looks a lot like the co's facade—fastidious, fuddy-duddy, thinking he knows what's best for others and trying to run their lives. He gets to look in a mirror, too, and it's not much fun for either of them. If they would both accept and respond to those parts of themselves that they're resisting, the mirrors would go away. What's more, they wouldn't even mind if the mirrors stayed around, because it would be no problem to look into them.

The purpose of that reflection is to get both people to see some things about themselves. If they don't see and respond to their "something wrong" in the person they're with now, one thing is certain: they'll have another chance with the next one.

THE ADVANTAGES OF CO-ISM

There must be some advantages to co-ism, or there wouldn't be so many people doing it. These are a few of the things people get out of being co's.

You never have to look at yourself.
When would you find time? You're always looking out for the addict who's taken the best years of your life. If it weren't for him, God knows what you could have accomplished. But as it is, you had no choice.

As I said, it doesn't even have to be an addict. It can be as simple as a husband who has to have breakfast cooked just right for him every morning. It can be your best friend who has arthritis, or your child who has bad grades. Almost anyone will do, because you can find a "problem" in almost anyone. There's a cornucopia of people out there, just waiting for a co!

There's always someone to blame.
Co-ism is made to order for victims. Not only do they get to play out their victimhood in spades, but it's undercover and people aren't nearly as likely to notice and call them on it!

You have an excuse for anything.
I once worked with a young man who had this one down pat. In this case, his child was the co.

In their household, the father would regularly get drunk and beat up his son Tommy, and then Tommy would run away from home. The pattern was as follows: Tommy would do something "good." He'd bring home a report card (all A's and one C), or jump into the middle of a family fight to protect his mother, or some other noble thing. However, his father always interpreted it as bad. His father would beat him up and Tommy would run away from home and hang out at one of his friends' houses.

There were several places where he stayed regularly. The friends' parents would invite him to stay for dinner, after which Tommy would just slip into the friend's room, unbeknown to the parents, and hide in the closet or under the bed—sometimes for days on end. He'd find places where he could sit around watching TV and eating candy bars and where he'd never have to do the dishes, or have any chores, or do his homework.

After a while he'd get bored and lonely, so he'd go home. He'd be grounded, of course, and there would be some tough rules laid down. Because they had grounded him, his parents felt guilty, so actually they ended up catering to him a little. They wanted to make up for punishing him and they didn't want him to run away again. Underneath the grounding and the rules, they were trying to score points with him. That would be fine for a while, but then amazingly enough, his father would get drunk again—right out of the blue—and beat him up. The pattern would repeat itself.

Tommy and I began to explore this "out of the blue" business and found out that it wasn't quite that way. Actually, after Tommy was home for a while, he'd start getting tired—of being restricted, of doing his chores, of trying to get good grades— tired of just about everything.

The next thing you know, he'd be showing his father the paper with the C rather than the one with the A. He'd be sure to step into a fight and protect his mother. He'd do anything to make sure his father was upset enough to get drunk and beat him up, so that he could run away. Tommy knew just where the buttons were. He made his father give him an excuse to leave.

In fact, he had an excuse to do just about anything he wanted. He was running the entire family!

People don't sit down and figure these things out ahead of time. It took Tommy quite a while to see what he was doing, and he wasn't happy when he *did* see it. The Robot is protecting itself. It knows somehow that if these schemes ever got to the conscious level, we might not accept them. In order to deal with co-ism, we have to be able to outsmart the Robot.

We can't do that by asking questions such as, "Well, am I really trying to bring about that person's downfall and keep him stuck so that I won't have to look at my own life?" No Robot is going to answer "Yes" to that. The place to look is at the results. Is the other person staying stuck? Is there always someone to blame? Is there an excuse for just about anything that happens in your life? If that victim role is starting to feel pretty real, it's time to look around and see if there's someone you are co-ing.

THE DISADVANTAGES OF CO-ISM

There is no freedom because
we are always attached.
If we need the alcoholic, we can't go anywhere he doesn't go. We can't live our own lives or pursue our own processes. Those things aren't available because we've sold them for the safety and protection from the unknown that co-ism provides.

There is no self-worth or self-esteem.
Self-worth comes in two ways. One is the ability to look yourself squarely in the eye and say, "I can trust myself; my code of ethics works for me and for others and I live by it; I make mistakes, but do my best to correct them. I am response-able." The second is watching yourself grow, seeing yourself become

a bigger person and experiencing more of yourself. Neither of these options is available to a co. Co's are afraid to look at their own process, and because they don't look at it or learn the lessons available to them, they don't grow.

All their value, as they see it, is tied up in being needed by the other person. By themselves, on their own with no one to care for, they are nothing.

There is almost no fun in life.

Co-ing is very serious business. If anybody started joking about it, they might just see through the co's whole scam. Not only that, but the situation is *tragic,* and it has to be kept that way. Once you start to introduce comedy into tragedy, tragedy doesn't last long. What if people thought this was *comic?* What if they laughed? The whole act would be blown.

HELPING KIDS TO OBSERVE THEIR CO-ISM

When there's an alcoholic in the family, children are often the ones closest to him or her, which puts them right in the line of fire for the abnormal behavior when it starts to surface—and in the perfect position to become co-alcoholics without realizing it. If children are aware of this possibility, then they will know that they have alternatives available to them and will be able to make choices in the situation.

If a child has an addict or an alcoholic in his life, he needs to know not to take their reactions personally. He needs to understand the nature of their illness and that they aren't doing hurtful things because they want to harm him, but because they believe their survival depends on keeping the substance in their system. He needs to know that the drug is causing both physical and psychological changes in the alcoholic.

Often the child doesn't understand that the parent is under

the influence. There are changes in behavior, and the child doesn't know what is going on, so quite often he attributes these changes to himself, whether changes are positive or negative.

The child needs to be able to identify when the addict or the alcoholic is under the influence or in withdrawal, and not take his or her behavior personally. It's also valuable for him to know that this is probably not the time to try to talk to the addict. It's better if he can wait until they aren't under the influence, so that there's a better chance that they will a) respond to him normally, and b) remember what is said. In cases where the alcoholic is always under the influence or in withdrawal, the best time to talk is when the mood is most mellow, possibly right after the first evening drink (or morning drink in some cases).

Children experience a lot of denial about their parents' alcoholism, not only because of the alcoholic's ability to hide his drinking, but also because of society's attitudes and the confusion they create. It's wrong to be a wino. The child's father doesn't look like a wino, so he couldn't be an alcoholic. But his father drinks, and that's what winos do. If his little friend says, "Boy, did your daddy get drunk at our house last night!" and drunk means being an alcoholic, and being an alcoholic means being a wino, then the child will defend his father to the death. He'll say his father did *not* drink, and deny it up and down.

Society often treats the children of alcoholics as if they were victims before they have a chance to deal with their situation. If the children get nothing but sympathy, attention, and excuses for their behavior, they're not going to be terribly interested in changing it.

They need to understand that they do have choices and that they are not powerless in the situation. They don't have to put up with having their baby-sitting money taken away. They don't have to put up with abuse—physical or emotional. If they take responsibility for their situation, then they create options for themselves.

It helps if you can explore some of those options with them. If they are living with an addict or alcoholic, they might want to join Alateen. If they are developing alcoholism or an addiction themselves, they can go to AA or to a treatment facility. The National Council on Alcoholism has an information and referral service for just about any situation involving alcohol.

You can also give them some guidelines for communicating with alcoholics and addicts. Basically, there are three things that work, and four things that don't work.

WHAT DOESN'T WORK

1. Lecturing
2. Pleading
3. Sympathizing
4. Arguing or fighting

WHAT WORKS

1. Duplicating their experience and
   having them duplicate yours.
2. Learning how to hear, not just to listen.
3. Learning how to be heard, not just to hear.

The most valuable gift you can give the child of an alcoholic is an opportunity to experience being in charge of their own life. By not falling into the trap of your own co-ism, by demonstrating that you are not the alcoholic's victim, you set an example for them. If they see you call a cab rather than drive with the alcoholic, and you give them cab money, then neither you nor they have to live in fear of a DWI accident. If you attend social events, do your job well, and have fun, they'll realize they can, too. If you discuss with them alternative locations or times for having their friends over, they can choose to do so. If you understand and explain the nature of alcoholism, and don't take it personally, they'll learn to do the same thing. Most of all, however, help them to get support through Alateen. If there is no chapter in your neighborhood, contact the national headquarters and learn how to set one up yourself. And if none of the above seems to work, then let go and leave it up to the child. After all, you wouldn't want to be a co!

PARENTS AS CO'S

If kids are in the perfect position to be co's, so are parents. The dynamic that takes place between parents and their children is a situation made to order for co-ism.

How many parents do you know who, to one extent or another, live their lives through or for their kids? There's nothing wrong with getting a charge out of your kids, doing things with them and loving them, but living your life through them is dangerous. It may create a very unhealthy relationship.

We want to do a good job as parents, and it's the ideal setup for co-ism. We want our children to be happy.

Add to this the highly charged issue of alcohol and other drugs and you have a powderkeg of co-ism. Alcohol and other drugs are things we *know* can hurt our kids, and we can get many sources of agreement on that point. We can become like tigers protecting their young where alcohol and other drugs are concerned.

HOW TO TELL IF YOU'RE
CO-ING YOUR CHILD

You can tell if you're co-ing your child is by listening to your communication patterns. The most outstanding feature of co's' communication is that they are judgmental. The second is that they are always right. They're so right they often spend a lot of time saying how willing they are to admit they're wrong.

Co's also plead, deny, beg, threaten, and withdraw their love. First they deny's there's a problem. Then they plead with the alcoholic and beg him not to drink. Failing that, they threaten him with something that will happen if he continues. If he goes ahead anyway, they simply withdraw. They retreat—but not for long. That would take them out of the game, so they'll be right back there pleading and begging at the start of the next round.

Here is a list of what works and what doesn't work when dealing with an alcoholic. It's taken from my booklet, *Facts about Booze and other Drugs.*

Doesn't work: Pleading, denying, begging, accusing, blaming, being sympathetic, covering up. ("He has the flu today, so he won't be in school.")

Doesn't work: Pouring booze down the sink, drinking with him, locking him in his room.

Doesn't work: Finding reasons for his drinking, such as "It's his mother's fault," "It's because of his math teacher," "It's her friends. They're a rough crowd," etc.

Doesn't work: Giving her some of your tranquilizers to calm her down; suggesting she try marijuana instead.

Doesn't work: Blaming the child for your problems; thinking that your troubles will stop as soon as he cleans up his act and stops worrying you; giving up and saying it's all useless.

Doesn't work: Saying that the situation is hopeless, but you've got to put up with it because your daughter will die without you.

Doesn't work: Sacrificing your life for your child either by being a "martyr" or a "stoic." Producing results in order to get approval for being a perfect parent, or *not* producing results in order to punish the people around you.

Works: Getting information for yourself about alcoholism through NCA, Alanon, Parents Who Care, AA.

Works: Learning that alcoholism is a physical disease and that you can't stop the alcoholic child from losing control. If she stops or slows down occasionally, remember she won't *stay stopped* because of anything you say or do. It has to come from her.

Works: Understanding that "reasons" prevent you and the alcoholic from seeing the truth, which is that alcoholism is a disease. As long as there are "reasons," the alcoholic will continue to try to drink in a controlled manner, and he will be more and more powerless to do this as the disease progresses. For example, if you've decided he drinks alcoholically because he never learned to read well, then he will continue to drink until he learns to read. This doesn't make sense!

Works: Knowing that alcoholics are easily addicted to any substance, and that other drugs (even prescription drugs) can be even more difficult for him to kick than booze. This means be very careful to research the treatment he may choose. Be sure that the doctors he goes to truly understand alcoholism as a disease!

Works: Finding a resource and some support for yourself so that you can find happiness for yourself, even though the alcoholic continues to drink. *It can be done.* Attend Alanon or family group therapy. Get involved in activities you gave up when your life became focused on your addicted child.

Works: Getting help for yourself so that you can stop trying to rescue the alcoholic and instead allow him to notice and take responsibility for his illness and its effects. Remember, your rescuing keeps him stuck.

Works: Producing results for the joy and satisfaction of doing so—because you *want* to, not because you have to prove something about yourself or your family.

LETTING GO OF BEING A CO

Letting go of being a co is one of the hardest things in the world. *It may be even harder to let go of being a co than it is for the alcoholic to stop drinking.* The first thing that comes up for both is all the reasons why they can't stop their destructive patterns.

Again, there is no "how to" let go of being a co. You just have to do it. It's not easy, but it's necessary. Remember, letting go means being willing to experience your child's pain. If you think he is in pain now, watch him when you start to pull back. He will think he's in even greater pain. The discomfort that comes of change and breaking down the homeostasis will be added to whatever else is going on with him.

Most people go back to the old patterns at this point, because they're afraid they're making the situation worse and might do permanent damage. They *are* making the situation worse, but unfortunately it has to get worse before it can get better. We call it tough love. And the sooner parents practice it the better. Doing your child's homework, blaming teachers for her failure, knowing she has stolen gum from the 5 and 10 and not making her return it, supporting her in finding reasons and excuses for her mistakes—this kind of protection will not provide the foundation to prepare her for facing and dealing with the consequences of drinking or drug use. The co has to love the alcoholic child enough to let him suffer the consequences of his behavior so that he can understand that there's a problem here and take whatever steps he needs to take to remedy the situation.

Beyond the discomfort of moving out of victimhood and into responsibility, both of you may start to feel all the emotions the situation has helped you stuff down until now. There may be sadness, grief, anger, resentment, and remorse. And one thing is certain—the child will blame it all on you. It will be your fault because you're deserting him, abandoning him. Now you're making his alcoholism worse, instead of helping him! Sound familiar? These are all the things you say about him.

They need you in this game as much as you need them, which makes it even more painful for you to pull away. You get to experience the pain of their pain as well as the pain of their blame! It's a big order, but one that may be the most important contribution you ever made to anyone, and you make it to yourself as well as to them.

WHAT TO DO IF YOU ARE A CO

Letting go is the first step, and it happens in substance rather than in form. As we've said before, it's a thing you *are,* a state you are in, rather than something you do. But there are things you can do as well. These are some of them:

Join Alanon.
Alanon works with co-alcoholics in much the same way Alcoholics Anonymous works with alcoholics. At Alanon, they don't sit around talking about the alcoholics, how irresponsible they are, or how to fix them. They talk about their own problems. It's a place where people give each other supportive feedback. They won't let you slide back into the victim syndrome.

Be willing to experience anything— because you may!
Here's where detachment is necessary. When you start to pull out of your role as co, both you and your child will be filled with strong emotions, guilt, and pain. If you try to go through that while you're still attached to him, you just might not make it. If you detach from him and from the situation, you'll come through with flying colors.

Stop blaming the child,
your parents, or society.

They didn't do it to you. Even if they did, blaming them wouldn't help or change the situation in any way. In order to get yourself out of this, you first have to recognize that you're the one who got yourself into it. Once you've done that, it's a lot easier to get yourself out. You take back the controls. If it's "their" fault, you have no power to change it. You're still concerned with how they are and what they do. Take back the power in your own life.

Take responsibility for the situation,
but don't take the blame.

Taking the blame for everything is the worst thing you could do. When you take responsibility, it's a statement that, "Yes, I'm contributing to this. I'm responsible. It's not bad; it's just what I did and I can change it now that I choose to do so." Taking blame means, "Oh no! I've done this terrible, awful thing that can probably never be fixed because I'm so bad and have ruined everyone's life!"

This will never produce the results you want. Taking blame for the situation is like the alcoholic taking a drink. It's the first step back to square one.

Co-ism is anything but hopeless. Recognize that it is an addiction, just as alcoholism is an addiction, and that you can let go of it as soon as you are willing to take the risk of living your own life and letting the alcoholic live his.

LIVING YOUR OWN LIFE

It sounds trite. Most people don't give it a second thought. It goes in one ear and out the other. Live your own life? Of course I'm living my own life! Everybody lives his own life!

That's not exactly what I mean. I mean living every day of your life as joyfully and completely as possible. I don't mean going through the motions, anesthetizing yourself with the routine, and thinking to yourself that it doesn't matter anyway because your family or your work are what are really important.

When I say living your life completely and joyfully as possible, I also mean holding the point of view that you and your well-being are the most important things in the world. Most people are appalled when they hear that. How selfish! They turn away and go back to their drudgery feeling very self-righteous. What they don't notice is that their lack of aliveness has a dramatic effect on the well-being (or lack of it) of everyone around them, including their children.

It's the old syndrome of, "I don't know why he isn't happy; I've given up everything for him." Well, one reason he isn't happy may be that he's living with an unhappy person. He's got a martyr sucking on his energy all the time. He'd probably rather have someone around who looked out for themselves, and was happy enough to contribute to the joy and fun of the relationship.

Sometimes it seems impossible even to consider the prospect of leading your own life. After all, so many people depend on you for so many things! You're so needed that if you stepped out of the pattern for one day the sky would probably fall in. Try it and see what happens. You may be surprised when, come nightfall, the sky is still up there and the walls of your house are still standing. Not only that, but everybody's having a wonderful time. It works even better when you tell them in advance that that's what you're going to do, so they can plan to make other arrangements for the things they've gotten used to your doing.

When was the last time you sat down and asked yourself these questions:

Why am I here on earth?

What are the things that are really important to me?

What are the three things I enjoy doing most?

When I'm eighty and looking back over my life, what do I want to have accomplished?

What kind of life would make me want to jump out of bed in the morning?

What are the things I want and need out of my relationships? Am I getting them?

Am I fulfilling all of my potential? If not, what would make me feel that I was?

Am I having any fun? If not, what can I do to have some fun?

Is there anything I haven't yet done that I want to make sure and do in life? When am I going to do it?

What are five things I could do to improve the quality of my life?

If you haven't thought about any of those questions in a while, you might want to do so. If you're a co, you surely want to do so. Living your own life means staying in touch with those questions, and making sure that the life you are leading is aligned with your answers to them.

You might find out that the way your life is right now isn't aligned with your answers. That's a little threatening, a little painful. But it's also the first step in getting the life and the answers lined up. You might have to be willing to step outside the boundaries you've imposed on your life. And you don't know how the people around you will react.

They'll probably react in one of two ways.

They will hate it. They'll try to shove you back into your place in the homeostasis, so that everything will be normal and predictable again. If that happens, you just have to be firm and remember that what you're doing will benefit them as well as you. If you stand on your own two feet and they see that you are the happier for it, they may even begin to come around—especially when they've all found their new places on the board and realized that what you did was a benefit to them as well.

They will love it. They'll be amazed at what a new and wonderful person you are, and won't be able to imagine why you didn't do it sooner. They'll find you fascinating, intriguing, and even more lovable than before. In this case, just enjoy.

CONSCIOUS DUPLICATION OF EXPERIENCE

The primary goal of this book is to aid you in the process of consciously duplicating your child's experience and making it possible for them to duplicate yours. To duplicate someone's experience means to actually feel what they feel—as if you are they. To do it consciously means to do it on purpose. Not because it was an accident. Not because of something they did. Not because the stars were in the right place. Not because you'd had enough sleep the night before. But because you chose to do it.

As we've seen, there are no rules for duplication. And there is no method. However, there are some guidelines. They have all been mentioned repeatedly throughout the book. And here is a summary of it all.

Hearing
The primary requirement for duplicating another's experience is the ability to hear—not just listen but actually hear. To hear means to become aware of or to be informed of.

Many people do not hear at all. They do listen. And they listen for one ultimate purpose—to agree, or rebut. If you only want to agree, or rebut, you didn't hear. You are simply waiting to impose your pictures on the other's experience, either through agreement or disagreement. Agreement and disagreement are reaction. Hearing is response.

Observation and experience.
In order to duplicate another's experience, you must observe your own. Your thoughts, feelings, attitudes, judgements, opinions—all are to be observed, experienced, and set aside until it's time to express them. Otherwise they will overpower your ability to truly hear. It may be that the time to express them is almost immediate. The point, however, is to observe them *first* before you verbalize them.

Intention-theirs.
To duplicate another's experience, you must hear "beyond" the words. You must know what the situation represents to them, and to yourself. Until you do that, you will be trying to communicate at the level of the issue. That won't work. You've got to communicate at the level of what the issue means to each of you.

Acknowledgment and restatement.
Acknowledge that you heard them. Without acknowledgment, the communication will not be complete. Acknowledgment does not mean "praise." It means recognition. And it is essential. Nothing is worse than trying to communicate in a vacuum, and that's what exists without acknowledgement.

Not only let them know that you hear, but tell them *what* you heard. If that isn't what they meant, ask them to restate it. Never do this in a challenging or combative way. After all, often one only becomes clear in the course of being heard. If you challenge or criticize someone, or say, "Well, if *that's* what you meant, why didn't you say it the first time," the communication is apt to come to a halt.

Expand your experience to include theirs.

This is the key to everything. Much communication is based on the fear of losing. "If I hear what they want, I'll have to give something up." Or, "if they actually heard me I'd know it because they'd be groveling at my feet right now doing exactly everything I want them to do." Obviously, that's not the result effective communication produces. Effective communication results in everyone ultimately winning.

SADD, or Students Against Driving Drunk, has designed a contract for teenagers and their parents concerning drinking and driving. The agreement is that teens will call their parents for a ride rather than drink and drive, or ride with a drunk driver. Parents agree to pick their children up and not get into a "discussion" on the night of the incident. Parents and teens who sign the contract are expanding their experience to include the others' experience. It is the only way to a satisfactory conclusion to most issues.

The idea behind the contract is that parents do not want their children drinking and driving. And, given the facts of today, there are apt to be times when such a situation could arise. SADD's contract addresses both experiences by acknowledging the parents' fears and, without condoning it, acknowledging the fact that many young people experiment with alcohol.

Intention—yours.

In order to have others hear you, or duplicate your experience, you also need to apply conscious intention.

Remember, what they heard is what you intended for them to hear. More than any words, what they will hear is your ground of being. And that's what they will react to.

Describe—don't evaluate.

Tell them *how you feel, not what they are.* Use all your senses.

Let them know what you see and hear; and what you have smelled, tasted and felt. Express, don't dump.

Be response-able.

Take responsibility for your thoughts and feelings and standards. Don't justify them, but do clarify them. Let your children know what they mean to you. Let them in on your cares, your concerns, your worries about them. Express what your experience is. Rather than, "You're such a reckless driver—and your drinking is really out of hand. How dare you even ask for the car to go to that beer bust?" try something closer to the truth. "I couldn't live with myself if you were injured in a Driving While Intoxicated incident. I know this seems like it's going to wreck your social life, but I just can't let you drive the car to that beer bust."

Expand your experience to include theirs.

Yes. I know I've already said this. And I'm saying it again. In order to be heard, you must include the experience of the hearer.

Find out if they heard what you meant. If they didn't, don't accuse them of being deaf, simply restate what you meant. Then be willing to hear their response. Explore alternatives with them. Perhaps the beer bust is out, but an alternative kind of party can be arranged in the near future. Maybe all they want right now is to make you wrong. Let them. If you resist, it will only get worse. If you expand your purpose to include theirs, they'll probably quit making you wrong as soon as they understand that it's okay with you.

Win/win

This is the ultimate goal. It may take time, but it will be worth it. There will be plenty of times when things definitely look like lose/lose. But hang in there and continue duplicating. The more you practice, the better you get.

Transformation

Relationships are continually in the process of transformation. There is a paradox here. We said at the beginning of this book that it might take years and years to unravel what it has taken ten or twenty or thirty years to build up. We said that commitment was the key, that you might have to keep at it for quite a while to establish the kind of communication you want with your children—about alcohol and other drugs, or anything else.

It's also true that transformation can happen in the twinkling of an eye. It can be (and often is) absolutely instantaneous. Sometimes all kids are waiting for is someone who isn't coming on to them like a parent, but as another person. As soon as they sense a human being, rather then a cardboard parent, on the other end of the communication, they can't wait to open up. If that's the case, it may happen overnight.

On the other hand, it may take a while, especially if the child is an addict, alcoholic, or co. But when you're communicating, you're never just waiting or "on hold." It may take you twenty years to achieve the kind of communication you want with your children, but every day of those twenty years you'll be learning something new about them and about yourself. Even if it's not going in exactly the direction you would like, or moving as quickly as you think it should, communication is constantly changing and growing. If you pay attention to it, you are constantly changing and growing, too.

There's no point in waiting. Those twenty years aren't going to pass any more quickly if you put them off. And you may discover that, for you, it happens overnight. Besides, remember that communication is a game in which the benefits start to accrue before you reach your goal. In communication, it's the trip and not the destination that counts.

Bibliography

Brecher, Edwards M. & the Editor of Consumer Reports. *Licit & Illicit Drugs*. Boston, Mass.: Little, Brown and Company, 1972.

Burack, Richard M.D. and Dr. Fred J. Fox. *The New Handbook of Prescription Drugs*. New York: Ballantine, rev. ed. 1975.

Goodwin, Donald. "Is Alcoholism Hereditary? A Review and Critique." *Archives of General Psychiatry,* 25 December 1971, pp. 545–549.

Goodwin, Alfred, Louis Gilman Goodman & Alfred Gilman (eds.) *The Pharmacological Basis of Therapeutics,* 6th ed. New York, N.Y.: MacMillan Publishing Co. Inc., 1980.

Hughes, Richard and Robert Brewin. *The Tranquilizing of America*. New York: Warner Books, 1979.

Jellinek, E. M. *The Disease Concept of Alcoholism*. New Haven, Conn.: Hillhouse Press, 1960.

Johnson, Vernon E. *I'll Quit Tomorrow*. New York: Harper and Row, 1973.

Kinney, Jean M.S.W. & Gwen Leaton. *Loosening the Grip, a Handbook of Alcohol Information*. Saint Louis, Mo.: C.V. Mosby Company, 1978.

Mann, Marty. *Marty Mann's New Primer on Alcoholism.* San Francisco: Rinehart and Winston, 1958.

Milam, James R. & Katherine Ketcham. *Under the Influence: A Guide to the Myths and Realities to Alcoholism.* Seattle: Madrona Publishers, Inc., 1981.

Saltman, Jules. "The new alcoholics: teenagers," *Public Affairs Pamphlet #499.* New York: Public Affairs Committee Inc., 1973.

Weil, Andrew M.D. & Winifred Rosen. *Chocolate to Morphine.* Boston, Mass.: Houghton Mifflin Co., 1983.

Williams, Roger J. *Alcoholism: The Nutritional Approach.* Austin: University of Texas Press, 1959.

Index